Europe
Through the Back Door
PHRASE BOOK

FRENCH

Rick Steves

John Muir Publications
Santa Fe, New Mexico

Thanks to the team of people at *Europe Through the Back Door* who helped make this book possible: Mary Carlson, Kendra Roth, Anne Kirchner, Margaret Berger, Colleen Murphy, Mary Romano, Plum Moore, Gene Openshaw and...

French translation: Scott Bernard, Paul Desloover
    and Steve Smith
Phonetics: Risa Laib
Layout: Rich Sorensen
Maps: Dave Hoerlein

Edited by Risa Laib and Rich Sorensen

John Muir Publications, P.O. Box 613, Santa Fe, NM 87504

ISBN 1-56261-091-0

Distributed to the book trade by
W.W. Norton & Company, Inc.
New York, NY

JMP travel guidebooks by Rick Steves:

2 to 22 Days in France (with Steve Smith)
Europe Through the Back Door
Europe 101: History and Art for the Traveler
  (with Gene Openshaw)
Mona Winks: Self-Guided Tours of Europe's Top Museums
  (with Gene Openshaw)
2 to 22 Days in Europe
2 to 22 Days in Great Britain
2 to 22 Days in Italy
2 to 22 Days in Germany, Austria & Switzerland
2 to 22 Days in Norway, Sweden & Denmark
2 to 22 Days in Spain & Portugal
Europe Through the Back Door Phrase Books:
  French, Italian and German
Asia Through the Back Door
Kidding Around Seattle

Rick Steves' company, *Europe Through the Back Door,*
provides many services for budget European travelers,
including a free quarterly newsletter/catalog, budget travel
books and accessories, Eurailpasses (with free video and
travel advice included), a free computer BBS Travel
Information Line, a travel partners list, intimate European bus
tours, and a user-friendly Travel Resource Center in
Edmonds, WA. For more information and a free newsletter
subscription, call or write to:

Europe Through the Back Door
109 Fourth Avenue N, Box 2009
Edmonds, WA 98020 USA
Tel: 206/771-8303, Fax: 206/771-0833
BBS: 206/771-1902 (1200-2400 baud, 8/N/1)

CONTENTS

Hi, I'm Rick Steves.

I'm the only mono-lingual speaker I know who's had the nerve to design a series of European phrase books. But that's one of the things that makes them better. You see, after twenty summers of travel through Europe, I've learned first-hand (1) what's essential for communication in another country, and (2) what's not. I've assembled these essential words and phrases in a logical, no-frills format, and I've worked with native Europeans and seasoned travelers to give you the simplest, clearest translations possible.

But this book is more than just a pocket translator. The words and phrases have been carefully selected to make you a happier, more effective budget traveler. The key to getting more out of every travel dollar is to get closer to the local people, and to rely less on entertainment, restaurants, and hotels that cater only to foreign tourists. This book will not only help you order a meal at a locals-only Parisian restaurant -- it will also help you discuss politics, social issues and other topics with the family that runs the place. Long after your memories of *chateaux* have faded, you'll still treasure the personal encounters you had with your new French friends.

A good phrase book should help you enjoy your French experience -- not just survive it -- so I've added a healthy dose of humor. But please use these phrases carefully, in a self-effacing spirit. Remember that one ugly American can undo the goodwill built by dozens of culturally-sensitive ones.

To get the most out of this book, take the time to

internalize and put into practice my French pronunciation tips. I've spelled out the pronunciations as if you were reading English. Don't worry too much about memorizing grammatical rules, like which gender a particular noun is -- the important thing is to communicate!

You'll notice this book has a tear-out "cheat sheet" section. Tear this out and keep it in your pocket, so you can easily use it to memorize key words and phrases during otherwise idle moments. You'll also find my *Rolling Rosetta Stone* word guide, and additional sections on French tongue-twisters, gestures, international words, and tips for using French telephones. As you prepare for your trip to France, you may want to have a look at my annually-updated *2 to 22 Days in France* guidebook.

One more thing that will help enrich your French experience is a basic understanding of French etiquette. This causes lots of needless frustration among Americans. Here's the situation in a nutshell: We Americans value informality as *friendliness*, and reject formality as *coldness*. To us, this seems natural. The French, on the other hand, value formality as *politeness*, and dismiss informality as *rudeness*. So ironically, the friendly, overly-familiar American and the subdued, just-the-facts-ma'am Frenchman are both trying hard to be *nice*, and they only succeed in offending one another. But remember, you are the outsider, so watch the locals and try to incorporate some French-style politeness into your routine. Walk into any shop in France and you will hear a cheery

"Bonjour, Monsieur / Madame." As you leave, you'll hear a lilting *"Au revoir, Monsieur / Madame."* Always address a man as *Monsieur*, a woman as *Madame*, and an unmarried young woman or a girl as *Mademoiselle* (leaving this out is like addressing a French person as "Hey, you!"). For good measure, toss in *s'il vous plaît* (please) whenever you can.

So adjust those cultural blinders. If you come to France expecting rudeness, you are sure to find it. If you respect the fine points of French culture and make an attempt to speak their language, you'll find the French -- in their uniquely French way -- as warm and friendly as any people in Europe.

My goal is to help you become a more confident, extroverted traveler. If this phrase book helps make that happen, or if you have suggestions for making it better, I'd love to hear from you.

Happy travels, and good luck as you hurdle the language barrier!

Rick Steves

Regions of France

Getting Started

Beautiful, challenging French

...is widely spoken outside of France. Half of Belgium
speaks French, and French rivals English as the
handiest second language in Spain, Portugal and Italy.
Even your US passport is translated into French.
You're probably already familiar with this poetic
language. Consider: *bonjour, c'est la vie, bon appétit,
merci, au revoir, bon voyage!*

As with any language, the key to communicating is
to go for it with a mixture of bravado and humility.
Try to sound like Maurice Chevalier or Inspector
Clouseau.

French has some unusual twists to its pronunciation:

Ç sounds like S in sun.
CH sounds like SH in shine.
G usually sounds like G in get.
But *G* followed by *E* or *I* sounds like S in treasure.
GN sounds like NI in onion.
H is always silent.
J sounds like S in treasure.
R sounds like a dry gargle.
I sounds like EE in seed.
É and *EZ* sound like AY in play.
When *ER* ends a word, it also sounds like AY in play.

French is tricky because the spelling and
pronunciation seem to have little to do with each

other. For example, *Qu'est-ce que c'est?* (What is that?) is pronounced: kehs kuh seh.

The final letters of many French words are silent, so *Paris* sounds like pah-ree. If a word ending in a consonant is followed by a word starting with a vowel, sometimes the consonant is linked with the vowel. *Mes amis* (my friends) sounds like may-zah-mee.

Le and *la* (the masculine and feminine "the") are connected to words starting with a vowel. *La orange* becomes *l'orange.*

Unlike English, Italian and German, the syllables of French words tend to be equally stressed.

French has a few sounds that are unusual in English: the French *u* and the nasal vowels. To say the French *u*, round your lips to say "oh," but say "ee." Vowels combined with either *n* or *m* are often nasal vowels. As you nasalize a vowel, let the sound come through your nose as well as your mouth. Remember, the vowel is the important thing. The *n* or *m,* represented here by n̲ for nasal, is not pronounced.

There are a total of four nasal sounds, all contained in the phrase *un bon vin blanc* (a good white wine).

Nasal vowels:		To make the sound:
un	uhn̲	nasalize the U in lung.
bon	ohn̲	nasalize the O in bone.
vin	an̲	nasalize the A in fantasy.
blanc	ahn̲	nasalize the A in want.

In phonetics, *un bon vin blanc* would read: uh<u>n</u> boh<u>n</u> va<u>n</u> blah<u>n</u>. Practice it, and you'll learn how to say the nasal vowels, and order a fine wine!

Here's a quick guide to the rest of the phonetics we've used in this book:

ah	like A in father.
ar	like AR in park.
ay	like AY in play.
eh	like E in let.
ee	like EE in seed.
ehr	sounds like "air."
ew	pucker your lips and say "ee."
g	like G in go.
or	like OR in core.
oh	like O in note.
oo	like OO in too.
s	like S in sun.
uh	like U in but.
ur	like UR in fur.
zh	like S in treasure.

French Basics

Meeting and greeting the French:

Good day.	**Bonjour.**	bohn-zhoor
Good morning.	**Bonjour.**	bohn-zhoor
Good evening.	**Bonsoir.**	bohn-swahr
Hi. (informal)	**Salut.**	sah-lew
Welcome!	**Bienvenue!**	bee-an-vuh-new
Mr.	**Monsieur**	muhs-yur
Mrs.	**Madame**	mah-dahm
Miss	**Mademoiselle**	mahd-mwah-zehl
How are you?	**Comment allez-vous?**	koh-mahn tah-lay voo
Very well, thanks.	**Très bien, merci.**	treh bee-an mehr-see
And you?	**Et vous?**	ay voo
My name is...	**Je m'appelle...**	zhuh mah-pehl
What's your name?	**Comment vous appelez-vous?**	koh-mahn voo zah-play-voo
Pleased to meet you.	**Enchanté.**	ahn-shahn-tay
Where are you from?	**D'où êtes-vous?**	doo eht voo
I am... / Are you...?	**Je suis... / Êtes-vous...?**	zhuh swee / eht-voo
...on vacation	**...en vacances**	zahn vah-kahns
...on business	**...en voyage d'affaires**	zahn voy-yahzh dah-fair
See you later.	**À bientôt.**	ah bee-an-toh
Goodbye.	**Au revoir.**	oh ruh-vwahr

| Good luck! | **Bonne chance!** | buhn shah<u>ns</u> |
| Have a good trip! | **Bon voyage!** | boh<u>n</u> voy-yahzh |

The top 50 survival phrases

Yes, you can survive in France using only these phrases. Most are repeated on your tear-out cheat sheet near the end of this book.

The ten essentials:

Good day.	**Bonjour.**	boh<u>n</u>-zhoor
Do you speak English?	**Parlez-vous anglais?**	par-lay-voo ah<u>n</u>-gleh
Yes.	**Oui.**	wee
No.	**Non.**	noh<u>n</u>
I don't understand.	**Je ne comprends pas.**	zhuh nuh koh<u>n</u>-prah<u>n</u> pah
I'm sorry.	**Désolé. / Je regrette.**	day-zoh-lay / zhuh ruh-greht
Please.	**S'il vous plaît.**	see voo pleh
Thanks.	**Merci.**	mehr-see
Thank you very much.	**Merci beaucoup.**	mehr-see boh-koo
Goodbye.	**Au revoir.**	oh ruh-vwahr

Where?

Where is...?	**Où est...?**	oo eh
...a hotel	**...un hôtel**	uh<u>n</u> oh-tehl
...a youth hostel	**...une auberge de jeunesse**	ewn oh-behrzh duh zhuh-nehs

...a restaurant	**...un restaurant**	uhn rehs-toh-rahn
...a grocery store	**...une épicerie**	ewn ay-pee-suh-ree
...the train station	**...la gare**	lah gar
...the tourist information office	**...l'office du tourisme**	loh-fees dew too-reez-muh
...the toilet	**...la toilette**	lah twah-leht
men / women	**hommes / dames**	ohm / dahm

How much?

How much does it cost?	**Combien?**	kohn-bee-an
Will you write it down?	**Pouvez-vous l'écrire?**	poo-vay-voo lay-kreer
Cheap. / Cheaper.	**Bon marché. / Moins cher.**	bohn mar-shay / mwan shehr
Included?	**Inclus?**	an-klew
I would like...	**Je voudrais...**	zhuh voo-dreh
We would like...	**Nous voudrions...**	noo voo-dree-ohn
Just a little. / More.	**Un petit peu. / Encore.**	uhn puh-tee puh / ahn-kor
A ticket.	**Un billet.**	uhn bee-yeh
A room.	**Une chambre.**	ewn shahn-bruh
The bill.	**L'addition.**	lah-dee-see-ohn

One through ten:

one	**un**	uh<u>n</u>
two	**deux**	duh
three	**trois**	trwah
four	**quatre**	kah-truh
five	**cinq**	sa<u>n</u>k
six	**six**	sees
seven	**sept**	seht
eight	**huit**	weet
nine	**neuf**	nuhf
ten	**dix**	dees

You'll find more numbers in the Numbers section on page 18.

Moving on:

I go to...	**Je vais à...**	zhuh veh ah
We go to...	**Nous allons à...**	noo zah-loh<u>n</u> ah
today	**aujourd'hui**	oh-zhoor-dwee
tomorrow	**demain**	duh-ma<u>n</u>
departure	**départ**	day-par
At what time?	**À quelle heure?**	ah kehl ur

What's up?

| Excuse me.
(to get attention) | **Pardon.** | par-doh<u>n</u> |
| Just a moment. | **Un moment.** | uh<u>n</u> moh-mah<u>n</u> |

It's a problem.	**C'est un problème.**	seh tuhn proh-blehm
It's good.	**C'est bon.**	seh bohn
Fantastic!	**Fantastique!**	fahn-tah-steek
You are very kind.	**Vous êtes très gentil.**	voo zeht treh zhahn-tee

Be creative! You can combine these phrases to say: "Two, please," or "No, thank you," or "I'd like a cheap hotel," or "Cheaper, please?" Please is a magic word in any language. If you want something and you don't know the word for it, just point and say, *"S'il vous plaît"* (Please). If you know the word for what you want, such as the bill, simply say, *"L'addition, s'il vous plaît"* (The bill, please).

Struggling with French:

Do you speak English?	**Parlez-vous anglais?**	par-lay-voo ahn-gleh
Even a teeny weeny bit?	**Un petit peu?**	uhn puh-tee puh
Please speak English.	**Parlez anglais, s'il vous plaît.**	par-lay ahn-gleh see voo pleh
You speak English well.	**Vous parlez bien anglais.**	voo par-lay bee-an ahn-gleh
I don't speak French.	**Je ne parle pas français.**	zhuh nuh parl pah frahn-seh
I speak a little French.	**Je parle français un petit peu.**	zhuh parl frahn-seh uhn puh-tee puh
I speak ten words in French.	**Je parle dix mots de français.**	zhuh parl dee moh duh frahn-seh

I study French.	**J'étudie le français.**	zhay-tew-dee luh frah<u>n</u>-seh
Excuse...	**Pardonnez...**	par-duh-nay
Correct...	**Corrigez...**	koh-ree-zhay
...my pronunciation.	**...ma prononclation.**	mah proh-noh<u>n</u>-see-ah-see-oh<u>n</u>
What is this in French?	**Comment dit-on en français?**	koh-mah<u>n</u> dee-toh<u>n</u> ah<u>n</u> frah<u>n</u>-seh
Repeat.	**Répétez.**	ray-pay-tay
Speak slowly.	**Parlez lentement.**	par-lay lah<u>n</u>-tuh-mah<u>n</u>
Excuse me? (didn't hear)	**Comment?**	koh-mah<u>n</u>
Do you understand?	**Comprenez-vous?**	koh<u>n</u>-pruh-nay-voo
I understand.	**Je comprends.**	zhuh koh<u>n</u>-prah<u>n</u>
I don't understand.	**Je ne comprends pas.**	zhuh nuh koh<u>n</u>-prah<u>n</u> pah
Will you write it down?	**Pouvez-vous l'écrire?**	poo-vay-voo lay-kreer
Does anybody here speak English?	**Y a-t-il quelqu'un qui parle anglais?**	ee ah-teel kehl-kuh<u>n</u> kee parl ah<u>n</u>-gleh

Common questions:

How much?	**Combien?**	koh<u>n</u>-bee-a<u>n</u>
How many?	**Combien?**	koh<u>n</u>-bee-a<u>n</u>
How long? (time)	**Combien de temps?**	koh<u>n</u>-bee-a<u>n</u> duh tah<u>n</u>
How?	**Comment?**	koh-mah<u>n</u>
Is it possible?	**C'est possible?**	seh poh-see-bluh
Is it far?	**C'est loin?**	seh lwa<u>n</u>

What?	**Quoi?**	kwah
What is that?	**Qu'est-ce que c'est?**	kehs kuh seh
What is better?	**Qu'est-ce qui est mieux?**	kehs kee eh mee-uh
When?	**Quand?**	kah<u>n</u>
What time is it?	**Quelle heure est-il?**	kehl ur eh-teel
At what time?	**À quelle heure?**	ah kehl ur
When does this...?	**Ça... à quelle heure?**	sah... ah kehl ur
...open	**...ouvre**	oo-vruh
...close	**...ferme**	fehrm
Do you have...?	**Avez-vous...?**	ah-vay-voo
Where is...?	**Où est...?**	oo eh
Where are...?	**Où sont...?**	oo soh<u>n</u>
Who?	**Qui?**	kee
Why?	**Pourquoi?**	poor-kwah
Why not?	**Pourquoi pas?**	poor-kwah pah

A statement or even a single word can turn into a question if you ask it in a questioning tone. *"C'est bon"* (It's good) becomes *"C'est bon?"* (Is it good?). *"Toilette?"* is an easy way to ask, "Where is the toilet?"

Yin and yang:

cheap / expensive	**bon marché / cher**	bohn mar-shay / shehr
big / small	**grand / petit**	grahn / puh-tee
hot / cold	**chaud / froid**	shoh / frwah
open / closed	**ouvert / fermé**	oo-vehr / fehr-may
entrance / exit	**entrée / sortie**	ahn-tray / sor-tee
arrive / depart	**arriver / partir**	ah-ree-vay / par-teer
early / late	**tôt / tard**	toh / tar
soon / later	**bientôt / plus tard**	bee-an-toh / plew tar
fast / slow	**vite / lent**	veet / lahn
here / there	**ici / là-bas**	ee-see / lah-bah
near / far	**près / loin**	preh / lwan
good / bad	**bon / mauvais**	bohn / moh-veh
best / worst	**le meilleur / le pire**	luh meh-yur / luh peer
a little / lots	**un peu / beaucoup**	uhn puh / boh-koo
more / less	**plus / moins**	plew / mwan
easy / difficult	**facile / difficile**	fah-seel / dee-fee-seel
beautiful / ugly	**beau (m), belle (f) / laid (m), laide (f)**	boh, behl / leh, lehd
intelligent / stupid	**intelligent / stupide**	an-teh-lee-zhahn / stew-peed
vacant / occupied	**libre / occupé**	lee-bruh / oh-kew-pay
with / without	**avec / sans**	ah-vehk / sahn

Little words that are big in France:

I	**je**	zhuh
you (formal)	**vous**	voo
you (informal)	**tu**	tew
he	**il**	eel
she	**elle**	ehl
we	**nous**	noo
and	**et**	ay
at	**à**	ah
but	**mais**	meh
by (via)	**par**	par
for	**pour**	poor
from	**de**	duh
not	**pas**	pah
now	**maintenant**	man-tuh-nahn
only	**seulement**	suhl-mahn
or	**ou**	oo
this / that	**ce / cette**	suh / seht
to	**à**	ah
very	**très**	treh

Handy French expressions:

Ça va?	sah vah	How are you? (informal)
Ça va.	sah vah	I'm fine. (response to **Ça va?**)
D'accord.	dah-kor	OK.
Comme ci, comme ça.	kohm see kohm sah	So so.
Formidable.	for-mee-dah-bluh	Great.

Voilà.	vwah-lah	Here is...
Bon appétit!	bohn ah-pay-tee	Enjoy your meal!
C'est comme ça.	seh kohm sah	That's the way it is.
Bon Dieu!	bohn dee-uh	Good God!

French names for places:

France	**la France**	lah frahns
French Riviera	**la Côte d'Azur**	lah koht dah-zewr
English Channel	**la Manche**	lah mahnsh
England	**l'Angleterre**	lahn-gluh-tehr
Netherlands	**les Pays-Bas**	lay peh-ee-bah
Germany	**l'Allemagne**	lahl-mahn-yuh
Switzerland	**la Suisse**	lah swees
Spain	**l'Espagne**	leh-spahn-yuh
Italy	**l'Italie**	lee-tah-lee
Greece	**la Grèce**	lah grehs
Europe	**l'Europe**	lur-rohp
United States	**les Etats-Unis**	lay zay-tah-zew-nee
world	**le monde**	luh mohnd

Numbers

French numbering is a little quirky from the seventies through the nineties. Let's pretend momentarily that the French speak English. Instead of saying 70, 71, 72, up to 79, the French say "sixty ten," "sixty eleven," "sixty twelve" up to "sixty nineteen." Instead of saying 80, the French say "four twenties." The numbers 81 and 82 are literally "four twenty one" and "four twenty two." It gets stranger. The number 90 is "four twenty ten." To say 91, 92, up to 99, the French say "four twenty eleven," "four twenty twelve" on up to "four twenty nineteen." But take heart. If little French children can learn these numbers, you can, too.

Numbers you can count on:

0	**zéro**	zay-roh
1	**un**	uhn
2	**deux**	duh
3	**trois**	trwah
4	**quatre**	kah-truh
5	**cinq**	sank
6	**six**	sees
7	**sept**	seht
8	**huit**	weet
9	**neuf**	nuhf
10	**dix**	dees
11	**onze**	ohnz
12	**douze**	dooz
13	**treize**	trehz

14	**quatorze**	kah-torz
15	**quinze**	kanz
16	**seize**	sehz
17	**dix-sept**	dee-seht
18	**dix-huit**	deez-weet
19	**dix-neuf**	deez-nuhf
20	**vingt**	van
21	**vingt et un**	vant ay uhn
22	**vingt-deux**	vant-duh
23	**vingt-trois**	vant-trwah
30	**trente**	trahnt
31	**trente et un**	trahnt ay uhn
40	**quarante**	kah-rahnt
41	**quarante et un**	kah-rahnt ay uhn
50	**cinquante**	san-kahnt
60	**soixante**	swah-sahnt
70	**soixante-dix**	swah-sahnt-dees
71	**soixante et onze**	swah-sahnt ay ohnz
72	**soixante-douze**	swah-sahnt-dooz
79	**soixante-dix-neuf**	swah-sahnt-deez-nuhf
80	**quatre-vingts**	kah-truh-van
81	**quatre-vingt-un**	kah-truh-van-uhn
90	**quatre-vingt-dix**	kah-truh-van-dees
91	**quatre-vingt-onze**	kah-truh-van-ohnz
92	**quatre-vingt-douze**	kah-truh-van-dooz
99	**quatre-vingt-dix-neuf**	kah-truh-van-deez-nuhf
100	**cent**	sahn
101	**cent un**	sahn uhn
102	**cent deux**	sahn duh
200	**deux cents**	duh sahn
1000	**mille**	meel
1994	**mille neuf cent**	meel nuhf sahn
	quatre-vingt-quatre	kah-truh-van-kah-truh

2000	**deux mille**	duh meel
10,000	**dix mille**	dee meel
1,000,000	**un million**	uhn meel-yohn
first	**premier**	pruhm-yay
second	**deuxième**	duhz-yehm
third	**troisième**	trwahz-yehm
half	**demi**	duh-mee
fifty percent	**cinquante pour cent**	san-kahnt poor sahn
number one	**numéro un**	new-may-roh uhn

Money

Key money words:

bank	**banque**	bah<u>n</u>k
money	**argent**	ar-zhah<u>n</u>
change money (v)	**changer de l'argent**	shah<u>n</u>-zhay duh lar-zhah<u>n</u>
exchange (n)	**bureau de change**	bew-roh duh shah<u>n</u>zh
traveler's check	**chèque de voyage**	shehk duh voy-yahzh
credit card	**carte de crédit**	kart duh kray-dee
cash advance	**crédit de caisse**	kray-dee duh kehs
cash machine	**distributeur de billets**	dee-stree-bew-tur duh bee-yeh
cashier	**caisse**	kehs
receipt	**reçu**	ruh-sew

Changing money:

Can you change dollars?	**Pouvez-vous changer les dollars?**	poo-vay-voo shah<u>n</u>-zhay lay doh-lar
What is your exchange rate for dollars...?	**Quel est le cours du dollar...?**	kehl eh luh koor dew doh-lar
...in traveler's checks	**...en chèques de voyage**	ah<u>n</u> shehk duh voy-yahzh
Are there extra fees?	**Y a-t-il d'autres frais?**	ee ah-teel doh-truh freh
What is the service charge?	**Quels sont les frais?**	kehl soh<u>n</u> lay freh

What is the commission?	**Quel est la commission?**	kehl eh lah koh-mee-see-oh<u>n</u>
I would like...	**Je voudrais...**	zhuh voo-dreh
...small bills.	**...les petits billets.**	lay puh-tee bee-yeh
...large bills.	**...les gros billets.**	lay groh bee-yeh
...coins.	**...les pièces.**	lay pee-ehs
...small change.	**...la petite monnaie.**	lah puh-teet muh-neh
I think you've made a mistake.	**Je crois que vous vous êtes trompés.**	zhuh krwah kuh voo voo zeht troh<u>n</u>-pay
I'm broke / poor / rich.	**Je suis fauché / pauvre / riche.**	zhuh swee foh-shay / poh-vruh / reesh
75 F	**soixante quinze francs**	swah-sah<u>nt</u> ka<u>n</u>z frah<u>n</u>
50 c	**cinquante centimes**	sa<u>n</u>-kah<u>n</u>t sah<u>n</u>-teem

French francs (F) are divided into 100 centimes (c). There are about 5 francs in a dollar, so divide prices in francs by 5 to get a rough estimate of the price in dollars.

Public Transportation

Tickets:

ticket	**billet**	bee-yeh
ticket office	**guichet**	gee-sheh
schedule	**horaire**	oh-rair
one way	**aller simple**	ah-lay san-pluh
roundtrip	**aller-retour**	ah-lay-ruh-toor
overnight	**nuit**	nwee
direct	**direct**	dee-rehkt
connection	**correspondance**	kor-rehs-pohn-dahns
first class	**première classe**	pruhm-yehr klahs
second class	**deuxième classe**	duhz-yehm klahs
reservation	**réservation**	ray-zehr-vah-see-ohn
seat	**place**	plahs
window seat	**place à la fenêtre**	plahs ah lah fuh-neh-truh
aisle seat	**place au couloir, à l'allée**	plahs oh kool-wahr, ah lah-lay
non-smoking	**non fumeur**	nohn few-mur
refund	**remboursement**	rahn-boor-suh-mahn

At the station:

arrival	**arrivée**	ah-ree-vay
departure	**départ**	day-par
delay	**retard**	ruh-tar

waiting room	**salle d'attente**	sahl dah-tah<u>nt</u>
check room	**consigne de bagages**	koh<u>n</u>-seen-yuh duh bah-gahzh
lockers	**consigne automatique**	koh<u>n</u>-seen-yuh oh-toh-mah-teek
baggage	**bagages**	bah-gahzh
lost and found office	**bureau des objets trouvés**	bew-roh day ohb-zheh troo-vay
tourist information	**office du tourisme**	oh-fees dew too-reez-muh

Trains:

French State Railways	**SNCF**	S N say F
train station	**gare**	gar
train information	**renseignements**	rah<u>n</u>-sehn-yuh-mah<u>n</u>
train	**train**	tra<u>n</u>
high-speed train	**TGV**	tay zhay vay
to the platforms	**accès aux quais**	ahk-seh oh kay
platform	**quai**	kay
track	**voie**	vwah
train car	**voiture**	vwah-tewr
dining car	**voiture restaurant**	vwah-tewr rehs-toh-rah<u>n</u>
sleeper car	**wagon-lit**	vah-goh<u>n</u>-lee
sleeper berth	**couchette**	koo-sheht
...upper	**...supérieure**	sew-pay-ree-ur
...middle	**...milieu**	meel-yuh
...lower	**...inférieure**	a<u>n</u>-fay-ree-ur
conductor	**conducteur**	koh<u>n</u>-dewk-tur

Buses:

bus station	**gare routière**	gar root-yehr
long distance bus	**car**	kar
city bus	**bus**	bews
bus stop	**arrêt de bus**	ah-reh duh bews

Boats:

boat	**bateau**	bah-toh
ferry	**bac, ferry**	bahk, fehr-ree
hydrofoil	**hydrofoil**	ee-droh-fwahl
barge	**péniche**	pay-neesh
cabin	**cabine**	kah-been

Subway:

subway	**métro**	may-troh
subway entrance	**l'entrée du métro**	lahn-tray dew may-troh
a book of subway tickets	**un carnet**	uhn kar-neh

When you're in Paris, buy a book of ten tickets for the subway. It's called a *carnet*, and will save you about 40%.

Train Route Map and Schedules

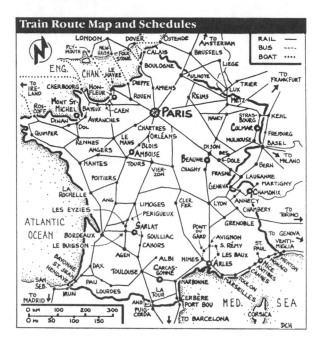

From	To	Length of trip	Approx. cost (2nd. class)
Paris	Nice	10 hrs.	$110
Paris	Avignon	6 hrs.	$70
Paris	Strasbourg	5 hrs.	$50
Paris	Brussels	3 hrs.	$40
Paris	Bordeaux	5 hrs.	$60
Paris	Lyon	4 hrs.	$45

Handy transportation phrases:

English	French	Pronunciation
How much is the fare to...?	**C'est combien pour...?**	seh kohn-bee-an poor
I'd like...	**Je voudrals...**	zhuh voo-dreh
...to go to ___.	**...aller à ___.**	ah-lay ah
...a ticket to ___.	**...un billet pour ___.**	uhn bee-yeh poor
Is a reservation required?	**Une réservation est-elle nécessaire?**	ewn ray-zehr-vah-see-ohn eh-tehl nay-suh-sair
I'd like to leave...	**Je voudrais partir...**	zhuh voo-dreh par-teer
I'd like to arrive...	**Je voudrais arriver...**	zhuh voo-dreh ah-ree-vay
...by ___.	**...à ___.**	ah
...in the morning.	**...le matin.**	luh mah-tan
...in the afternoon.	**...l'après-midi.**	lah-preh-mee-dee
...in the evening.	**...le soir.**	luh swahr
Is there a...?	**Y a-t-il un...?**	ee ah-teel uhn
...earlier departure	**...départ plus tôt**	day-par plew toh
...later departure	**...départ plus tard**	day-par plew tar
...supplement	**...supplément**	sew-play-mahn
...cheaper ticket	**...bIllet moins cher**	bee-yeh mwan shehr
When is the next departure?	**Le prochain départ est à quelle heure?**	luh proh-shan day-par eh tah kehl ur
Will you write it down?	**Pouvez-vous l'écrire?**	poo-vay-voo lay-kreer
Where does it leave from?	**Il part d'où?**	eel par doo
On what track?	**Sur quelle voie?**	sewr kehl vwah
When will it arrive?	**Il va arriver à quelle heure?**	eel vah ah-ree-vay ah kehl ur

Is it direct?	**C'est direct?**	seh dee-rehkt
Must I transfer?	**Faut-il que je fasse une correspondance?**	foh-teel duh zhuh fahs ewn kor-rehs-pohn-dahns
When? / Where?	**À quelle heure? / Où?**	ah kehl ur / oo
Which train to...?	**Quel train pour...?**	kehl tran poor
Which train car to...?	**Quelle voiture pour...?**	kehl vwah-tewr poor
Which bus to...?	**Quel bus pour...?**	kehl bews poor
Does it stop at...?	**Est-ce qu'il s'arrête à...?**	ehs keel sah-reht ah
Is this seat free?	**Cette place est libre?**	seht plahs eh lee-bruh
That's my seat.	**C'est ma place.**	seh mah plahs
Save my place.	**Gardez ma place.**	gar-day mah plahs
Where are you going?	**Où allez-vous?**	oo ah-lay-voo
I'm going to...	**Je vais à...**	zhuh veh ah
Can you tell me when to get off?	**Pouvez-vous m'indiquer mon arrêt?**	poo-vay-voo man-dee-kay mohn ah-reh

If you're on a train and you spot a cute town, get off
and explore, and use the same ticket to continue your
journey on a later train.

Reading train and bus schedules:

à, pour	to
arrivée	arrival
de	from
départ	departure
dimanche	Sunday
jour férié	holiday
jours	days

jusqu'à	until
la semaine	weekdays
samedi	Saturday
sauf	except
seulement	only
tous	every
tous les jours	daily
vacances	holidays

French schedules use the 24-hour clock. It's like American time until noon. After that, subtract twelve and add p.m. So 13:00 is 1 p.m., 20:00 is 8 p.m., and 24:00 is midnight. Train travelers take note: if your train is scheduled to depart at 00:01, it'll leave one minute after midnight.

Taking taxis:

taxi	**taxi**	tahk-see
Where is a taxi stand?	**Une station de taxi?**	ewn stah-see-ohn duh tahk-see
Are you free?	**Libre?**	lee-bruh
Occupied.	**Occupé.**	oh-kew-pay
How much will it cost to go to...?	**C'est combien pour aller à...?**	seh kohn-bee-an poor ah-lay ah
Too much.	**Trop.**	troh
How many people can you take?	**Combien de passagers pouvez-vous prendre?**	kohn-bee-an duh pah-sah-zhay poo-vay-voo prahn-druh

Is there an extra fee?	**Y a-t-il un supplément?**	ee ah-teel uh<u>n</u> sew-play-mah<u>n</u>
The meter, please.	**Le compteur, s'il vous plaît.**	luh koh<u>n</u>-tur see voo pleh
The most direct route.	**La route la plus directe.**	lah root lah plew dee-rehkt
Slow down.	**Ralentissez.**	rah-lah<u>n</u>-tee-say
If you don't slow down, I'll throw up.	**Si vous ne ralentez pas, je vais vomir.**	see voo nuh rah-lah<u>n</u>-tay pah, zhuh veh voh-meer
Stop here.	**Arrêtez là.**	ah-reh-tay lah
Can you wait?	**Pouvez-vous attendre?**	poo-vay-voo zah-tah<u>n</u>-druh
I'll never forget this ride.	**Je ne vais jamais oublier cette promenade.**	zhuh nuh veh zhah-meh oo-blee-yay seht prohm-nahd
Where did you learn to drive?	**Où avez-vous appri à conduire?**	oo ah-vay-voo ah-pree ah koh<u>n</u>-dweer
I'll only pay what's on the meter.	**Je paie seulement ce qui est indiqué.**	zhuh peh suhl-mah<u>n</u> suh kee eh ta<u>n</u>-dee-kay
My change, please.	**La monnaie, s'il vous plaît.**	lah muh-neh see voo pleh
Keep the change.	**Gardez la monnaie.**	gar-day lah muh-neh

So you'll know what to expect, you can ask about typical taxi fares at the tourist information office. Taxi drivers always charge for loading baggage in the trunk.

Driving

Wheeling and dealing:

I'd like to rent...	**Je voudrais louer...**	zhuh voo-dreh loo-ay
...a car.	**...une voiture.**	ewn vwah-tewr
...a motorcycle.	**...une motocyclette.**	ewn moh-toh-see-kleht
...a motor scooter.	**...un vélomoteur.**	uhn vay-loh-moh-tur
...a bicycle.	**...un vélo.**	uhn vay-loh
...the Concorde.	**...le Concorde.**	luh kohn-kord
How much per...?	**Combien par...?**	kohn-bee-an par
...hour	**...heure**	ur
...day	**..jour**	zhoor
...week	**...semaine**	suh-mehn

Gassing up:

gas station	**station service**	stah-see-ohn sehr-vees
self-service	**libre service**	lee-bruh sehr-vees
Where is the nearest gas station?	**La plus proche station service?**	lah plew prohsh stah-see-ohn sehr-vees
Fill the tank.	**Faites le plein.**	feht luh plan
I need...	**Il me faut...**	eel muh foh
...gas.	**...essence.**	eh-sahns
...unleaded.	**...sans plomb.**	sahn plohn
...regular.	**...normale.**	nor-mahl
...super.	**...super.**	sew-pehr

...diesel.	**...gazole.**	gah-zoyl
...oil.	**...de l'huile.**	duh lweel
Check...	**Vérifiez...**	vay-ree-fee-ay
...the oil.	**...l'huile.**	lweel
...the air in the tires.	**...l'air dans les pneus.**	lair dahn lay puh-nuh
...the water.	**...l'eau.**	loh
...the radiator.	**...le radiateur.**	lah rahd-yah-tur
...the battery.	**...la batterie.**	lah bah-tuh-ree
...the fuses.	**...les fusibles.**	lay few-zee-bluh
...the fanbelt.	**...la courroie du ventilateur.**	lah koor-wah dew vahn-tee-lah-tur
...the brakes.	**...les freins.**	lay fran

The cheapest gas in France is sold in *hypermarché*
(supermarket) parking lots. Rather than dollars and
gallons, pumps will read francs and liters (basically 5
francs in a dollar, and 4 liters in a gallon).

Car trouble:

accident	**accident**	ahk-see-dahn
breakdown	**en panne**	ahn pahn
funny noise	**bruit curieux**	brwee kew-ree-uh
electrical problem	**problème d'électricité**	proh-blehm day-lehk-tree-see-tay
It won't start.	**Il ne veut pas partir.**	eel nuh vuh pah par-teer
This doesn't work.	**Ça ne marche pas.**	sah nuh marsh pah
It's overheating.	**Il surchauffe.**	eel sewr-shohf

I need a...	Il me faut un...	eel muh foh uhn
...tow truck.	...dépanneur.	day-pah-nur
...mechanic.	...mécanicien.	may-kah-nee-see-an
...stiff drink.	...bon coup.	bohn koo
Can you fix it?	Pouvez-vous le réparer?	poo-vay-voo luh ray-pah-ray
Just do the essentials.	Ne faites que le minimum.	nuh feht kuh luh mee-nee-muhm
When will it be ready?	Quand sera-t-elle prête?	kahn suh-rah-tehl preht
How much will it cost to make it run?	Combien pour la faire marcher?	kohn-bee-an poor lah fair mar-shay
I'm going to faint.	Je vais m'évanouir.	zhuh veh may-vahn-weer

Parking:

parking garage	garage	gah-rahzh
Where can I park?	Où puis-je me garer?	oo pwee-zhuh muh gah-ray
Is parking nearby?	Y a-t-il un parking près d'ici?	ee ah-teel uhn par-keeng preh dee-see
Can I park here?	Puis-je me garer ici?	pwee-zhuh muh gah-ray ee-see
How long can I park here?	Je peux me garer ici pour combien de temps?	zhuh puh muh gah-ray ee-see poor kohn-bee-an duh tahn
Must I pay to park here?	Dois-je payer pour me garer ici?	dwah-zhuh pay-yay poor muh gah-ray ee-see
Is this a safe place to park?	C'est prudent de me garer ici?	seh prew-dahn duh muh gah-ray ee-see

Bike bits:

bicycle	**vélo**	vay-loh
tire	**pneu**	puh-nuh
inner tube	**chambre à air**	shahn-bruh ah air
wheel	**roue**	roo
spoke	**rayon**	rah-yohn
chain	**chaîne**	shehn
freewheel	**roue libre**	roo lee-bruh
shifter	**levier de vitesse**	luhv-yehr duh vee-tehs
brakes	**freins**	fran
I brake for bakeries.	**Je m'arrête à chaque boulangerie.**	zhuh mah-reht ah shahk boo-lahn-zhuh-ree

Finding Your Way

Key navigation words:

straight ahead	**tout droit**	too dwah
left / right	**à gauche / à droite**	ah gohsh / ah dwaht
first / next	**premier / prochain**	pruhm-yay / proh-sha<u>n</u>
intersection	**carrefour**	kar-foor
stoplight	**feu**	fuh
square	**place**	plahs
street	**rue**	rew
bridge	**pont**	poh<u>n</u>
tunnel	**tunnel**	tew-nehl
overpass	**passerelle**	pah-suh-rehl
underpass	**passage sous-terrain**	pah-sahzh soo-tehr-ra<u>n</u>
highway	**grande route**	grah<u>n</u>d root
national highway	**route nationale**	root nah-see-oh-nahl
freeway	**autoroute**	oh-toh-root
road map	**carte**	kart
city map	**plan**	plah<u>n</u>

The shortest distance between any two points is the *autoroute*, but the tolls add up. You'll travel cheaper, but slower, on a *route nationale*.

Getting directions:

I am going to...	**Je vais à...**	zhuh veh ah
How do I get to...?	**Comment aller à...?**	koh-mah<u>n</u> tah-lay ah
How many minutes...?	**Combien de minutes...?**	koh<u>n</u>-bee-a<u>n</u> duh mee-newt
...on foot	**...à pied**	ah pee-yay
...by car	**...en voiture**	ah<u>n</u> vwah-tewr
How many kilometers to...?	**Combien de kilometres à...?**	koh<u>n</u>-bee-a<u>n</u> duh kee-loh-meh-truh ah
What's the... route to ___?	**Quelle est la... route pour ___?**	kehl eh lah... root poor
...best	**...meilleure**	meh-yur
...fastest	**...plus directe**	plew dee-rehkt
...most interesting	**...plus intéresssante**	plew za<u>n</u>-tay-reh-sah<u>n</u>t
Point it out on the map.	**Indiquez sur cette carte.**	a<u>n</u>-dee-kay sewr seht kart
I'm lost.	**Je suis perdu.**	zhuh swee pehr-dew
Where am I?	**Où suis-je?**	oo swee-zhuh
Who am I?	**Qui suis-je?**	kee swee-zhuh
Where is...?	**Où est...?**	oo eh
Where is the nearest...?	**Le plus proche...?**	luh plew prohsh
Where is this address?	**Où se trouve cette adresse?**	oo suh troov seht ah-drehs

Reading road signs:

attention travaux	workers ahead
céder le passage	yield
centre ville	to the center of town
déviation	detour
entrée	entrance
péage	toll
ralentir	slow down
réservé aux piétons	pedestrians only
sens unique	one-way street
sortie	exit
stationnement interdit	no parking
stop	stop
toutes directions	out of town (all directions)
virages	curves

On some major thoroughfares, you'll see electronic signs flashing messages to let you know what's ahead: *bouchon* (traffic jam), *circulation* (traffic), and *fluide* (no traffic). If you see the flashing lights of a patrol car, practice this handy phrase: *"Pardon, je suis touriste."* (Sorry, I'm a tourist.)

Other signs you may see:

à louer	for rent or for hire
à vendre	for sale
dames	women
danger	danger
défence de fumer	no smoking
défence de toucher	do not touch
défence d'entrer	keep out
eau non potable	undrinkable water
entrée libre	free admission
entrée interdite	no entry
fermé	closed
fermé pour restauration	closed for restoration
fermeture annuelle	closed for vacation
guichet	ticket window
hommes	men
interdit	forbidden
occupé	occupied
ouvert	open
ouvert de... à...	open from... to...
prudence	caution
sortie de secours	emergency exit
toilettes	toilets
WC	toilet

Telephones

Key telephone words:

Post, Telephone & Telegraph Office	**PTT**	pay tay tay
telephone	**téléphone**	tay-lay-fohn
operator	**standardiste**	stahn-dar-deest
international assistance	**renseignements internationaux**	rahn-sehn-yuh-mahn an-tehr-nah-see-oh-noh
country code	**code international**	kohd an-tehr-nah-see-oh-nahl
area code	**code régional**	kohd ray-zhee-oh-nahl
phone card	**télécarte**	tay-lay-kart
telephone book	**bottin**	boh-tan
yellow pages	**pages jaunes**	pahzh zhohn
toll-free	**gratuit**	grah-twee
out of service	**hors service**	or sehr-vees

Handy phone phrases:

Where is the nearest phone?	**Le plus proche téléphone?**	luh plew prohsh tay-lay-fohn
It doesn't work.	**Il ne marche pas.**	eel nuh marsh pah
Where is the PTT?	**Où est le PTT?**	oo eh luh pay tay tay
I'd like to telephone the USA.	**Je voudrais téléphoner aux USA.**	zhuh voo-dreh tay-lay-foh-nay oh zew ehs ah

What is the cost per minute?	**C'est combien par minute?**	seh koh<u>n</u>-bee-a<u>n</u> par mee-newt
I'd like to make a... call.	**Je voudrais faire un appel...**	zhuh voo-dreh fair uh<u>n</u> ah-pehl
...local	**...local.**	loh-kahl
...collect	**...en P.C.V.**	ah<u>n</u> pay say vay
...credit card	**...avec carte de crédit.**	ah-vehk kart duh kray-dee
...person to person	**...avec préavis.**	ah-vehk pray-ah-vee
...long distance (within France)	**...interurbain.**	a<u>n</u>-tehr-ewr-ba<u>n</u>
...international	**...international.**	a<u>n</u>-tehr-nah-see-oh-nahl
May I use your phone?	**Puis-je téléphoner?**	pwee-zhuh tay-lay-foh-nay
Can you dial for me?	**Pouvez-vous composer le numéro?**	poo-vay-voo koh<u>n</u>-poh-zay luh new-may-roh
Can you talk for me?	**Pouvez-vous parler pour moi?**	poo-vay-voo par-lay poor mwah
It's busy.	**C'est occupé.**	seh oh-kew-pay
Will you try again?	**Essayez de nouveau?**	eh-seh-yay duh noo-voh
Hello.	**Âllo.**	ah-loh
My name is...	**Je m'appelle...**	zhuh mah-pehl
My number is...	**Mon numéro est...**	moh<u>n</u> new-may-roh eh
Speak slowly and clearly.	**Parlez lentement et clairement.**	par-lay lah<u>n</u>-tuh-mah<u>n</u> ay klair-mah<u>n</u>
Wait a moment.	**Un moment.**	uh<u>n</u> moh-mah<u>n</u>
Don't hang up.	**Ne racrochez pas.**	nuh rah-kroh-shay pah

Use the handy French *télécarte* instead of coins to make phone calls. You can can buy a *télécarte* at post offices, train stations and *tabac* (tobacco) shops. Insert the card into a phone and call anywhere in the world. See "Let's Talk Telephones" later in this book for important French telephone tips and numbers.

Finding a Room

If you keep it very simple and use these phrases, you will be able to reserve a hotel room over the phone. A good time to reserve a room is the morning of the day you plan to arrive. You'll find related phrases in the Telephone and Time sections.

Key room-finding words:

hotel	**hôtel**	oh-tehl
small hotel	**pension**	pahn-see-ohn
room in a home	**chambre d'hôte**	shahn-bruh doht
youth hostel	**auberge de jeunesse**	oh-behrzh duh zhuh-nehs
room	**chambre**	shahn-bruh
people	**personnes**	pehr-suhn
night	**nuit**	nwee
arrive	**arriver**	ah-ree-vay
today	**aujourd'hui**	oh-zhoor-dwee
tomorrow	**demain**	duh-man
vacancy	**chambre libre**	shahn-bruh lee-bruh
no vacancy	**complet**	kohn-pleh

Handy hotel-hunting phrases:

I'd like to reserve a room...	**Je voudrais réserver une chambre...**	zhuh voo-dreh ray-zehr-vay ewn shahn-bruh
Do you have a room...?	**Avez-vous une chambre...?**	ah-vay-voo ewn shahn-bruh
...for one person / two people	**...pour une personne / deux personnes**	poor ewn pehr-suhn / duh pehr-suhn
...for tonight	**...pour ce soir**	poor suh swahr
...for two nights	**...pour deux nuits**	poor duh nwee
...for this Monday	**...pour lundi**	poor luhn-dee
...for Monday, August 28	**...pour lundi, le vingt-huit août**	poor luhn-dee luh van-tweet oot
with / without / and	**avec / sans / et**	ah-vehk / sahn / ay
...a toilet	**...un WC**	uhn vay say
...a shower	**...une douche**	ewn doosh
...a private bathroom	**...une salle de bains**	ewn sahl duh ban
...a double bed	**...un grand lit**	uhn grahn lee
...twin beds	**...lits jumeaux, duex petits lits**	lee zhew-moh, duh puh-tee lee
...a view	**...une vue**	ewn vew
...only a sink	**...un lavabo seulement**	uhn lah-vah-boh suhl-mahn
How much does it cost?	**Combien?**	kohn-bee-an

You may hear: *"Je regrette"* (I'm sorry). *"L'hôtel est complet"* (The hotel is full). Or, *"Vous devez arriver avant seize heures"* (You must arrive before 16:00).

Working out the details:

My name is...	**Je m'appelle...**	zhuh mah-pehl
I'm coming now.	**J'arrive tout de suite.**	zhah-reev tood sweet
I'll arrive in one hour.	**Je vais arriver dans une heure.**	zhuh veh ah-ree-vay dah<u>n</u> zewn ur
I'll arrive before 16:00.	**Je vais arriver avant seize heures.**	zhuh veh ah-ree-vay ah-vah<u>n</u> sehz ur
We arrive Monday, depart Wednesday.	**Nous arrivons lundi, nous partons mercredi.**	noo zah-ree-voh<u>n</u> luh<u>n</u>-dee, noo par-toh<u>n</u> mehr-kruh-dee
I have a reservation.	**J'ai une réservation.**	zhay ewn ray-zehr-vah-see-oh<u>n</u>
Confirm my reservation.	**Confirmez mes réservations.**	koh<u>n</u>-feer-may may ray-zehr-vah-see-oh<u>n</u>
I'll sleep anywhere. I'm desperate.	**Je vais dormir n'importe où. Je suis désespéré.**	zhuh veh dor-meer na<u>n</u>-por too. zhuh swee day-zuh-spay-ray
I have a sleeping bag.	**J'ai un sac de couchage.**	zhay uh<u>n</u> sahk duh koo-shahzh
How much is your cheapest room?	**Combien pour la chambre la moins chère?**	koh<u>n</u>-bee-a<u>n</u> poor lah shah<u>n</u>-bruh lah mwa<u>n</u> shehr
Is it cheaper if I stay three nights?	**C'est moins cher si je reste trois nuits?**	seh mwa<u>n</u> shehr see zhuh rehst trwah nwee
I'll stay three nights.	**Je vais rester trois nuits.**	zhuh veh rehs-tay trwah nwee
Breakfast included?	**Petit déjeuner compris?**	puh-tee day-zhuh-nay koh<u>n</u>-pree

Is breakfast required?	**Le petit déjeuner est obligatoire?**	luh puh-tee day-shuh-nay eh toh-blee-gah-twahr
How much without breakfast?	**Combien sans le petit déjeuner?**	kohn-bee-an sahn luh puh-tee day-zhuh-nay
Complete price?	**Prix tout compris?**	pree too kohn-pree
Service included?	**Service compris?**	sehr-vees kohn-pree
Can I see the room?	**Puis-je voir la chambre?**	pwee-zhuh vwahr lah shahn-bruh
Show me another room.	**Montrez-moi une autre chambre.**	mohn-tray-mwah ewn oh-truh shahn-bruh
Do you have something...?	**Avez-vous quelque chose de...?**	ah-vay-voo kehl-kuh shohz duh
...larger / smaller	**...plus grand / moins grand**	plew grahn / mwan grahn
...better / cheaper	**...meilleur / moins cher**	meh-yur / mwan shehr
...in the back / quieter	**...derrière / plus tranquille**	dehr-yehr / plew trahn-keel
No, thank you.	**Non, merci.**	nohn mehr-see
This is good.	**C'est bien.**	seh bee-an
I'll take it.	**Je la prends.**	zhuh lah prahn
My key, please.	**Le clé, s'il vous plaît.**	luh klay see voo pleh
Sleep well.	**Dormez bien.**	dor-may bee-an
Good night.	**Bonne nuit.**	buhn nwee

In French hotels, the first floor isn't the ground floor -- it's one floor above the ground floor. The second floor is two above the ground floor, and so on.

Hotel help and hassles:

I'd like...	**Je voudrais...**	zhuh voo-dreh
...clean sheets.	**...les draps propres.**	lay drah proh-pruh
...a pillow.	**...un oreiller.**	uhn oh-reh-yay
...a blanket.	**...une couverture.**	ewn koo-vehr-tewr
...a towel.	**...une serviette de bain.**	ewn sehrv-yeht duh ban
...toilet paper.	**...le papier hygiénique.**	luh pahp-yay ee-zhay-neek
...a crib.	**...une berceau.**	ewn behr-soh
...a small extra bed.	**...un lit de camp.**	uhn lee duh kahn
...a roll-away bed.	**...un lit pliant.**	uhn lee plee-ahn
...silence.	**...silence.**	see-lahns
Is there an elevator?	**Un ascenseur?**	uhn ah-sahn-sur
Come with me.	**Venez avec moi.**	vuh-nay ah-vehk mwah
I have a problem in my room.	**J'ai un problème dans ma chambre.**	zhay uhn proh-blehm dahn mah shahn-bruh
bad odor	**mauvaise odeur**	moh-vehz oh-dur
bugs	**insectes**	an-sehkt
mice	**souris**	soo-ree
prostitutes	**prostituées**	proh-stee-tew-ay
The bed is too soft / hard.	**Le lit est trop mou / dur.**	luh lee eh troh moo / dewr
I'm covered with bug bites.	**Je suis couvert de piqures de punaise.**	zhuh swee koo-vehr duh pee-kewr duh pew-nehz
There is no hot water.	**Il n'y a plus d'eau chaude.**	eel nee yah plew doh shohd

When is the water hot?	**L'eau sera chaude à quelle heure?**	loh suh-rah shohd ah kehl ur
Where can I wash / hang my laundry?	**Où puis-je faire / étendre ma lessive?**	oo pwee-zhuh fair / ay-tahn-druh mah luh-seev
I'd like to stay another night.	**Je voudrais rester encore une nuit.**	zhuh voo-dreh rehs-tay ahn-kor ewn nwee
Where shall I park?	**Je me gare où?**	zhuh muh gar oo
What time do you lock up?	**Vous fermez à quelle heure?**	voo fehr-may ah kehl ur
What time is breakfast?	**Le petit déjeuner est servi à quelle heure?**	luh puh-tee day-zhuh-nay eh sehr-vee ah kehl ur
Wake me at 7:00.	**Réveillez-moi à sept heures.**	ray-veh-yay-mwah ah seht ur

If you'd rather not struggle all night with a log-style French pillow, most hotels store a fluffier American-style pillow in the closet, as well as an extra blanket.

Checking out:

I'll leave...	**Je vais partir...**	zhuh veh par-teer
We'll leave...	**Nous allons partir...**	noo zah-lohn par-teer
...today / tomorrow.	**...aujourd'hui / demain.**	oo-zhoor-dwee / duh-man
When is check-out time?	**Quelle est l'heure limite d'occupation?**	kehl eh lur lee-meet doh-kew-pah-see-ohn
Can I pay now?	**Puis-je régler la note?**	pwee-zhuh ray-glay lah noht
The bill, please.	**La note, s'il vous plaît.**	lah noht see voo pleh

Can I pay with a credit card?	**Acceptez-vous les cartes de crédit?**	ahk-sehp-tay-voo lay kart duh kray-dee
I slept like a baby.	**J'ai dormi comme un enfant.**	zhay dor-mee kohm uhn ahn-fahn
Everything was great.	**C'était super.**	say-teh sew-pehr
Can I leave my bag here...?	**Puis-je laisser ma valise ici...?**	pwee-zhuh leh-say mah vah-leez ee-see
Can we leave our bags here...?	**Pouvons-nous laisser nos valises ici...?**	poo-vohn-noo leh-say noh vah-leez ee-see
...until ___	**... jusqu'à ___**	zhews-kah

Camping:

Where is the nearest campground?	**Le plus proche camping?**	luh plew prohsh kahn-peeng
Can I...?	**Puis-je...?**	pwee-zhuh
Can we...?	**Pouvons-nous...?**	poo-vohn-noo
...camp here for one night	**...camper ici pour une nuit**	kahn-pay ee-see poor ewn nwee
Are showers included?	**Les douches inclus?**	lay doosh an-kloo
shower token	**jeton**	zhuh-tohn

In some French campgrounds and youth hostels you must buy a *jeton* (token) to activate a coin-operated hot shower. It has a timer inside, like a parking meter. To avoid a sudden cold rinse, buy at least two *jetons* before getting undressed.

Eating

Finding a restaurant:

Where's a good... restaurant?	**Où se trouve un bon restaurant...?**	oo suh troov uhn bohn rehs-toh-rahn
...cheap	**...bon marché**	bohn mar-shay
...local-style	**...cuisine régionale**	kwee-zeen ray-zhee-oh-nahl
...untouristy	**...pas touristique**	pah too-ree-steek
...Chinese	**...chinois**	sheen-wah
...fast food	**...fast food**	fahst food

Ordering meals:

What would you like?	**Que voulez-vous?**	kuh voo-lay voo
I'd like...	**Je voudrais...**	zhuh voo-dreh
...a table for two.	**...une table pour deux.**	ewn tah-bluh poor duh
...non-smoking.	**...non fumeur.**	nohn few-mur
...just a drink.	**...une consommation seulement.**	ewn kohn-soh-mah-see-ohn suhl-mahn
...a snack.	**...un snack.**	uhn snahk
...to see the menu.	**...voir la carte.**	vwahr lah kart
...to order.	**...commander.**	koh-mahn-day
...to eat.	**...manger.**	mahn- zhay
...to pay.	**...payer.**	pay-yay
...to throw up.	**...vomir.**	voh-meer

What do you recommend?	**Qu'est-ce que vous suggérez?**	kehs kuh voo sewg-zhay-ray
What's your favorite?	**Quel est votre favorit?**	kehl eh voh-truh fah-voh-ree
Is it...?	**C'est...?**	seh
...good	**...bon**	bohn
...expensive	**...cher**	shehr
...light	**...léger**	lay-zhay
...filling	**...copieux**	kohp-yuh
What's cheap and filling?	**Qu'est-ce qu'il y a de bon marché et de copieux?**	kehs kee lee yah duh bohn mar-shay ay duh kohp-yuh
What is fast?	**Qu'est-ce qui est déjà préparé?**	kehs kee eh day-zhah pray-pah-ray
What is local?	**Qu'est-ce que vous avez de la région?**	kehs kuh voo zah-vay duh lah ray-zhee-ohn
What is that?	**Qu'est-ce que c'est?**	kehs kuh seh
Do you have...?	**Avez-vous...?**	ah-vay-voo
...an English menu	**...une carte en anglais**	ewn kart ahn ahn-gleh
...a children's portion	**...une assiette d'enfant**	ewn ahs-yeht dahn-fahn

Dietary restrictions:

| I'm allergic to... | **Je suis allergique à...** | zhuh swee zah-lehr-zheek ah |
| I cannot eat... | **Je ne mange pas de...** | zhuh nuh mahnzh pah duh |

...dairy products.	**...produits laitiers.**	proh-dwee leh-tee-yay
...fat.	**...gras.**	grah
...meat.	**...viande.**	vee-ahnd
...salt.	**...sel.**	sehl
...sugar.	**...sucre.**	sew-kruh
I'm a diabetic.	**Je suis diabétique.**	zhuh swee dee-ah-bay-teek
No alcohol.	**Sans alcool.**	sahn zahl-kohl
I am a...	**Je suis...**	zhuh swee
...vegetarian.	**...végétarien.**	vay-zhay-tah-ree-an
...strict vegetarian.	**...végétarien rigoureux.**	vay-zhay-tah-ree-an ree-goo-ruh
...carnivore.	**...carnivore.**	kar-nee-vor

While the slick self-service restaurants are easy to use, you'll often eat better for the same money in a good little family bistro.

Key menu words:

breakfast	**petit déjeuner**	puh-tee day-zhuh-nay
lunch	**déjeuner**	day-zhuh-nay
dinner	**dîner**	dee-nay
menu of the day	**menu du jour**	muh-new dew zhoor
special of the day	**plat du jour**	plah dew zhoor
specialty of the house	**spécialité de la maison**	spay-see-ah-lee-tay duh lah meh-zohn
tourist menu	**menu touristique**	muh-new too-ree-steek

fixed price	**prix fixe**	pree feeks
appetizers	**hors-d'oeuvre**	or duh-vruh
soup	**soupe**	soop
salad	**salade**	sah-lahd
bread	**pain**	pan
first course	**entrée**	ahn-tray
main course	**le plat principal**	luh plah pran-see-pahl
meat	**viande**	vee-ahnd
poultry	**volaille**	voh-leh-ee
seafood	**fruits de mer**	frwee duh mehr
side dishes	**à la carte**	ah lah kart
vegetables	**légumes**	lay-gewm
dessert	**dessert**	duh-sehr
beverages	**boissons**	bwah-sohn
beer	**bière**	bee-ehr
wine	**vin**	van
cover charge	**couvert**	koo-vehr
service included	**service compris**	sehr-vees kohn-pree
service not included	**service non compris**	sehr-vees nohn kohn-pree
with / and / or / without	**avec / et / ou / sans**	ah-vehk / ay / oo / sahn

French cuisine is sightseeing for your tastebuds. Restaurants normally serve from 12:00 to 14:00, and from 19:00 until about 22:00. The menu is posted right on the front door or window, and "window shopping" for your meal is a fun, important part of the experience. Many cafés have a cheap *plat du jour* special for lunch. Most places offer fixed-price menus *(prix fixe)* which give you several choices for each course offered. *Service compris (s.c.)* means that the tip is included in the price. There's no need to tip beyond that. For a complete language guide, travel with the excellent Marling French Menu Master.

Restaurant requests and regrets:

A little.	**Un peu.**	uhn puh
More.	**Encore.**	ahn-kor
Another.	**Un autre.**	uhn oh-truh
I did not order this.	**Ce n'est pas ce que j'ai commandé.**	suh neh pah suh kuh zhay kohm-mahn-day
Is it included with the meal?	**C'est inclus avec le repas?**	seh an-kloo ah-vehk luh ruh-pah
I'm in a hurry.	**Je suis pressé.**	zhuh swee preh-say
I have an appointment at...	**J'ai rendez-vous à...**	zhay rahn-day-voo ah
Will the food be ready soon?	**Ce sera prêt bientôt?**	suh suh-rah preh bee-an-toh
I've changed my mind.	**J'ai changé d'avis.**	zhay shahn-zhay dah-vee
Can I get it "to go?"	**Pour emporter?**	poor ahn-por-tay
This is...	**C'est...**	seh
...delicious.	**...délicieux.**	day-lee-see-uh
...dirty.	**...sale.**	sahl
...too greasy.	**...trop graisseux.**	troh greh-suh
...too salty.	**...trop salé.**	troh sah-lay

...undercooked.	**...pas assez cuit.**	pah ah-say kwee
...overcooked.	**...trop cuit.**	troh kwee
...inedible.	**...immangeable.**	a<u>n</u>-mah<u>n</u>-zhah-bluh
...cold.	**...froid.**	frwah
Can you heat this up?	**Pouvez-vous faire réchauffer ceci?**	poo-vay-voo fair ray-shoh-fay suh-see
Yuk! (while turning your head away)	**Pouah!**	pwah
Do any of your customers return?	**Avez-vous des clients qui reviennent?**	ah-vay-voo day klee-ah<u>n</u> kee ruh-vee-a<u>n</u>
Enough.	**Assez.**	ah-say
Finished.	**Terminé.**	tehr-mee-nay
The food was magnificent.	**Le repas était magnifique.**	luh ruh-pah ay-teh mahn-yee-feek
My compliments to the chef!	**Mes compliments au chef!**	may koh<u>n</u>-plee-mah<u>n</u> oh shehf

Paying for your meal:

Waiter.	**Garçon.**	gar-soh<u>n</u>
Waitress.	**Mademoiselle.**	mahd-mwah-zehl
The bill, please.	**L'addition, s'il vous plaît.**	lah-dee-see-oh<u>n</u> see voo pleh
Together. / Separate checks.	**Ensemble. / Notes séparées.**	ah<u>n</u>-sah<u>n</u>-bluh / noht say-pah-ray
Can I pay with a credit card?	**Acceptez-vous les cartes de crédit?**	ahk-sehp-tay-voo lay kart duh kray-dee
Is there a cover charge?	**Y a-t-il un couvert?**	ee ah-teel uh<u>n</u> koo-vehr

Is service included?	**Le service est compris?**	luh sehr-vees eh koh<u>n</u>-pree
This is not correct.	**Ce n'est pas exact.**	suh neh pah ehg-zahkt
Can you explain this?	**Pouvez-vous expliquer ceci?**	poo-vay-voo zehk-splee-kay suh-see
What if I wash the dishes?	**Si je lave la vaiselle moi-même?**	see zhuh lahv lah veh-sehl mwah-mehm
Keep the change.	**Gardez la monnaie.**	gar-day lah muh-neh
This is for you.	**C'est pour vous.**	seh poor voo

What's on the table:

table	**table**	tah-bluh
plate	**assiette**	ahs-yeht
napkin	**serviette**	sehrv-yeht
knife	**couteau**	koo-toh
fork	**fourchette**	foor-sheht
spoon	**cuillère**	kwee-yehr
glass	**verre**	vehr
carafe	**carafe**	kah-rahf
water	**de l'eau**	duh loh

Edible extras:

bread	**pain**	pa<u>n</u>
butter	**beurre**	bur
margarine	**margarine**	mar-gah-reen
salt	**sel**	sehl
pepper	**poivre**	pwah-vruh
sugar	**sucre**	sew-kruh
honey	**miel**	mee-ehl

mustard	**moutarde**	moo-tard
mayonnaise	**mayonnaise**	mah-yuh-nehz
ketchup	**ketchup**	"ketchup"
olives	**olives**	oh-leev
pickles	**cornichons**	kor-nee-shohn
garlic	**ail**	ah-ee
oil	**huile**	weel
vinegar	**vinaigre**	vee-neh-gruh

What's for breakfast:

breakfast	**petit déjeuner**	puh-tee day-zhuh-nay
eggs	**des oeufs**	day zuh
fried eggs	**oeufs au plat**	uh oh plah
scrambled eggs	**oeufs brouillés**	uh broo-yay
boiled egg	**oeuf à la coque**	uhf ah lah kohk
soft / hard	**mollet / dur**	moh-leh / dewr
omelette	**omelette**	oh-muh-leht
ham	**jambon**	zhahn-bohn
cheese	**fromage**	froh-mahzh
roll	**petit pain**	puh-tee pan
toast	**toast**	tohst
butter	**beurre**	bur
jelly	**confiture**	kohn-fee-tewr
pastry	**pâtisserie**	pah-tee-suh-ree
croissant	**croissant**	kwah-sahn
yogurt	**yaourt**	yah-oort
cereal	**céréale**	say-ray-ahl
milk	**lait**	leh

hot cocoa	**chocolat chaud**	shoh-koh-lah shoh
fruit juice	**jus de fruit**	zhew duh frwee
orange juice (fresh)	**jus d'orange (frais)**	zhew doh-rah<u>nz</u>h (freh)
tea / lemon	**thé / citron**	tay / see-troh<u>n</u>
coffee (see Drinking)	**café**	kah-fay
Is breakfast included in the room cost?	**Est-ce que le petit déjeuner est compris?**	ehs kuh luh puh-tee day-zhuh-nay eh koh<u>n</u>-pree

French hotel breakfasts are expensive and often optional. They normally include a good cup of coffee (no refills), and a fresh *croissant* or a chunk of *baguette* with butter and jelly. Being a juice and cheese man, I keep a liter box of OJ in my room for a morning eye-opener and a wedge of "Laughing Cow" cheese in my bag for a moo-vable feast. You can also save money by breakfasting at a *bar* or *café*, where it's acceptable to bring in a croissant from the neighboring *boulangerie*.

Snacks:

snack	**snack**	snahk
sandwich	**sandwich**	sah<u>nd</u>-weech
crepe	**crêpe**	krehp
buckwheat crepe	**galette**	gah-leht
omelet	**omelette**	oh-muh-leht
quiche...	**quiche...**	keesh
...with cheese	**...au fromage**	oh froh-mahzh

...with ham	**...au jambon**	oh zhah<u>n</u>-boh<u>n</u>
...with mushrooms	**...aux champignons**	oh shah<u>n</u>-peen-yoh<u>n</u>
...with bacon, cheese and onions	**...lorraine**	lor-rehn
paté	**pâté**	pah-tay
toasted ham and cheese sandwich	**croque monsieur**	krohk muhs-yur
toasted ham, cheese & fried egg sandwich	**croque madame**	krohk mah-dahm

Light meals are quick and easy at *cafés* and *bars* throughout France. A *sandwich, crêpe, quiche* or *omelette* is a fairly cheap way to fill up, even in Paris. Each can be made with various extras like ham, cheese, mushrooms, and so on. *Crêpes* come in dinner or dessert varieties.

Soups and salads:

soup	**soupe, potage**	soop, poh-tahzh
clear soup	**consommé**	koh<u>n</u>-soh-may
broth	**bouillon...**	boo-yoh<u>n</u>
...chicken	**...de poulet**	duh poo-leh
...beef	**...de boeuf**	duh buhf
...with noodles	**...aux nouilles**	oh noo-ee
...with rice	**...au riz**	oh ree
thick vegetable soup	**potage de légumes**	poh-tahzh duh lay-gewm
onion soup	**soupe à l'oignon**	soop ah lohn-yoh<u>n</u>

shellfish chowder	**bisque**	beesk
seafood stew	**bouillabaisse**	boo-yah-behs
green salad	**salade verte**	sah-lahd vehrt
chef's salad	**salade composée**	sah-lahd kohn-poh-zay
mixed salad	**salade mixte**	sah-lahd meekst
lettuce	**laitue**	leh-tew
tomatoes	**tomates**	toh-maht
cucumber	**concombre**	kohn-kohn-bruh
no / a little / more	**non / un peu / encore**	nohn / uhn puh / ahn-kor
oil / vinegar	**huile / vinaigre**	weel / vee-neh-gruh
salad dressing	**vinaigrette**	vee-neh-greht
dressing on the side	**la sauce à part**	lah sohs ah par
What is in this salad?	**Qu'est-ce qu'il y a dans cette salade?**	kehs kee lee yah dahn seht sah-lahd

Restaurants normally serve only a *vinaigrette* dressing, though sometimes you'll find oil and vinegar on the table.

Seafood:

seafood	**fruits de mer**	frwee duh mehr
assorted sea-food	**assiette de fruits de mer**	ahs-yeht duh frwee duh mehr
fish	**poisson**	pwah-sohn
cod	**cabillaud**	kah-bee-yoh
cod (salty)	**morue**	moh-rew

salmon	**saumon**	soh-moh<u>n</u>
trout	**truite**	trweet
tuna	**thon**	toh<u>n</u>
herring	**hareng**	ah-rah<u>n</u>
anchovies	**anchois**	ah<u>n</u>-shwah
mussels	**moules**	mool
oysters	**huîtres**	wee-truh
shrimp	**crevettes**	kruh-veht
prawns	**scampi**	skah<u>n</u>-pee
crab	**crabe**	krahb
lobster	**homard**	oh-mar
squid	**calmar**	kahl-mar
Where did this live?	**D'où est-ce que ça vient?**	doo ehs kuh sah vee-a<u>n</u>

Poultry and meat:

poultry	**volaille**	voh-leh-ee
chicken	**poulet**	poo-leh
turkey	**dinde**	dan<u>d</u>
duck	**canard**	kah-nar
meat	**viande**	vee-ah<u>n</u>d
beef	**boeuf**	buhf
roast beef	**rosbif**	rohs-beef
beef steak	**bifteck**	beef-tehk
ribsteak	**entrecôte**	ah<u>n</u>-truh-koht
meat stew	**ragoût**	rah-goo

veal	**veau**	voh
cutlet	**côtelette**	koh-tuh-leht
pork	**porc**	por
ham	**jambon**	zhahn-bohn
horse	**cheval**	shuh-vahl
lamb	**agneau**	ahn-yoh
bunny	**lapin**	lah-pan
snails	**escargots**	ehs-kar-goh
frog legs	**cuisses degrenouilles**	kwees duh greh-noo-ee
brains	**cervelle**	sehr-vehl
sweetbreads	**ris de veau**	ree duh voh
tongue	**langue**	lahng
liver	**foie**	fwah
How long has this been dead?	**Il est mort depuis longtemps?**	eel eh mor duh-pwee lohn-tahn

How it's prepared:

hot	**chaud**	shoh
cold	**froid**	frwah
raw	**cru**	krew
cooked	**cuit**	kwee
baked	**cuit au four**	kwee oh foor
boiled	**bouilli**	boo-yee
fillet	**filet**	fee-leh
fresh	**frais**	freh
fried	**frit**	free
grilled	**grillé**	gree-yay
microwave	**four à micro-ondes**	foor ah mee-kroh-ohnd
mild	**doux**	doo

poached	**poché**	poh-shay
roasted	**rôti**	roh-tee
sautéed	**sauté**	soh-tay
smoked	**fumé**	few-may
spicy hot	**piquant**	pee-kahn
steamed	**à la vapeur**	ah lah vah-pur
stuffed	**farci**	far-see

Avoiding mis-steaks:

raw (hamburger steak)	**tartare**	tar-tar
very rare (quick contact with grill)	**bleu**	bluh
rare	**saignant**	sehn-yahn
medium	**à point**	ah pwan
well-done	**bien cuit**	bee-an kwee
almost burnt	**très bien cuit**	treh bee-an kwee

French specialties:

boeuf bourguignon	beef stew cooked with wine, bacon, onions and mushrooms
cassoulet	meat and beans casserole
choucroute garni	Alsacian sauerkraut with sausages, ham and potatoes
coq au vin	chicken cooked with wine, bacon, onions and mushrooms
pâté de foie gras	goose liver paté

steak tartare	raw ground beef (usually served with raw egg)
tournedos	thick slice of fillet
ratatouille	casserole of eggplant, zucchini, tomatoes, onions and green peppers
salade niçoise	salad with lettuce, tuna, tomatoes, olives, anchovies and hard-boiled eggs

French cooking styles and sauces:

aioli	garlic mayonnaise
Anglaise	boiled
Béarnaise	sauce of egg yolks, butter, tarragon, white wine and shallots
beurre blanc	sauce of butter, white wine and shallots
Bourguignon	cooked in red wine
forestière	with mushrooms
gratiné	topped with melted cheese and bread crumbs
Hollandaise	sauce of butter and egg yolks
jardinière	with vegetables
meunière	coated with flour and fried in butter
Normande	cream sauce
Provençale	with tomatoes, garlic, olive oil and herbs
nouvelle cuisine	a blend of fresh ingredients -- appealing, low in fat, and very expensive

Veggies, rice and pasta:

vegetables	**légumes**	lay-gewm
mixed vegetables	**légumes variés**	lay-gewm vah-ree-ay
with vegetables	**garni**	gar-nee
raw veggies	**crudités**	krew-dee-tay
artichoke	**artichaut**	ar-tee-shoh
asparagus	**asperges**	ah-spehrzh
beans	**haricots**	ah-ree-koh
beets	**betterave**	beh-teh-rahv
broccoli	**brocoli**	broh-koh-lee
cabbage	**chou**	shoo
carrots	**carottes**	kah-roht
cauliflower	**chou-fleur**	shoo-flur
corn	**maïs**	mah-ees
eggplant	**aubergine**	oh-behr-zheen
green beans	**haricots verts**	ah-ree-koh vehr
green peppers	**poivrons verts**	pwah-vrohn vehr
leeks	**poireaux**	pwah-roh
mushrooms	**champignons**	shahn-peen-yohn
onions	**oignons**	ohn-yohn
peas	**pois**	pwah
spinach	**épinards**	ay-pee-nar
zucchini	**courgette**	koor-zheht
potato	**pomme de terre**	pohm duh tehr
French fries	**pommes frites**	pohm freet
rice	**riz**	ree
pasta	**pâtes**	paht
spaghetti	**spaghetti**	spah-geh-tee

Say cheese:

cheese	**fromage**	froh-mahzh
brie	**brie**	bree
goat	**chèvre**	shev-ruh
bleu cheese	**fromage bleu**	froh-mahzh bluh
mild cheese	**fromage doux**	froh-mahzh doo
cream cheese	**fromage à la crème**	froh-mahzh ah lah krehm
Swiss cheese	**gruyère**	grew-yehr
Laughing Cow	**La vache qui rit**	lah vahsh kee ree
cheese board	**le plâteau de fromages**	luh plah-toh duh froh-mahzh
May I taste a little?	**Je peux goûter un peu?**	zhuh puh goo-tay uh<u>n</u> puh

In France, the cheese course is served just before (or instead of) dessert. It not only helps with the digestion, but gives the traveler a great opportunity to sample the excellent regional cheeses.

French fruit:

fruit	**fruit**	frwee
apple	**pomme**	pohm
apricot	**abricot**	ah-bree-koh
banana	**banane**	bah-nahn
berries	**baies**	beh
cherry	**cerise**	suh-reez
coconut	**noix de coco**	nwah duh koh-koh
date	**datte**	daht

fig	**figue**	feeg
grapefruit	**pamplemousse**	pahn-pluh-moos
grapes	**raisins**	reh-zan
lemon	**citron**	see-trohn
melon	**melon**	muh-lohn
orange	**orange**	oh-rahnzh
peach	**pêche**	pehsh
pear	**poire**	pwahr
pineapple	**ananas**	ah-nah-nah
plum	**prune**	prewn
prune	**pruneau**	prew-noh
raspberry	**framboise**	frahn-bwahz
strawberry	**fraise**	frehz
tangerine	**mandarine**	mahn-dah-reen
watermelon	**pastèque**	pah-stehk

Nuts to you:

almond	**amande**	ah-mahnd
chestnut	**marron, chataîgne**	mah-rohn, shah-tehn
hazelnut	**noisette**	nwah-zeht
peanut	**cacahuete**	kah-kah-weet
walnut	**noix**	nwah

French treats:

dessert	**dessert**	duh-sehr
cake	**gâteau**	gah-toh
ice cream	**glace**	glahs
scoop of ice cream	**coupe**	koop
sherbet	**sorbet**	sor-beh
fruit cup	**salade de fruits**	sah-lahd duh frwee
tart	**tartelette**	tar-tuh-leht
pie	**tarte**	tart
whipped cream	**crème chantilly**	krehm shahn-tee-yee
mousse	**mousse**	moos
custard	**crème caramel**	krem kar-ah-mehl
meringues in custard	**île flottante**	eel floh-tahnt
pastry	**pâtisserie**	pah-tee-suh-ree
fruit pastry	**chausson**	shoh-sohn
croissant with chocolate	**pain au chocolat**	pan oh shoh-koh-lah
buttery cake	**madeleine**	mah-duh-lehn
crepes	**crêpes**	krehp
cookies	**petits gâteaux**	puh-tee gah-toh
candy	**bonbons**	bohn-bohn
low calorie	**bas en calories**	bah ahn kah-loh-ree
homemade	**fait à la maison**	feh ah lah meh-zohn
Exquisite!	**Exquis!**	ehk-skee

Drinking

Water, milk and juice:

mineral water	**eau minérale**	oh mee-nay-rahl
(non) carbonated	**(non) gazeuse**	(nohn) gah-zuhz
tap water	**l'eau du robinet**	loh dew roh-bee-neh
whole milk	**lait entier**	leh ahnt-yay
skim milk	**lait écrémé**	leh ay-kray-may
fresh milk	**lait frais**	leh freh
hot chocolate	**chocolat chaud**	shoh-koh-lah shoh
fruit juice	**jus de fruit**	zhew duh frwee
orange juice	**jus d'orange**	zhew doh-rahnzh
apple juice	**jus de pomme**	zhew duh pohm
hard apple cider	**cidre**	see-druh
with /	**avec /**	ah-vehk /
without ice	**sans glaçons**	sahn glah-sohn
glass / cup	**verre / tasse**	vehr / tahs
small bottle	**petite bouteille**	puh-teet boo-teh-ee
large bottle	**grande bouteille**	grahnd boo-teh-ee
Is the water safe to drink?	**L'eau est potable?**	loh eh poh-tah-bluh

At a restaurant, you'll get free tap water with your meal if you say, *"L'eau du robinet, si'l vous plaît."* If you prefer mineral water, *Evian* and *Vittel* are two popular brands without carbonation. *Badoit* is a brand with carbonation. The half-liter plastic water-bottles with screw tops are light and sturdy -- great to pack along and re-use as you travel.

Coffee and tea:

coffee	**café**	kah-fay
espresso	**express**	"express"
American-style	**café américain**	kah-fay ah-may-ree-kan
½ coffee and ½ milk	**café au lait**	kah-fay oh leh
instant coffee	**Nescafé**	"Nescafé"
decaffeinated, decaf	**dé-caffiné, déca**	day-kah-fee-nay, day-kah
black coffee	**café noir**	kah-fay nwahr
coffee with cream	**café crème**	kah-fay krehm
sugar	**sucré**	sew-kray
hot water	**l'eau chaude**	loh shohd
tea / lemon	**thé / citron**	tay / see-trohn
tea bag	**sachet de thé**	sah-sheh duh tay
herbal tea	**tisane**	tee-zahn
small / big	**petit / grand**	puh-tee / grahn
Another cup.	**Encore une tasse.**	ahn-kor ewn tahs

Every *café* or *bar* has a complete price list posted.
You'll notice prices are listed in ascending order for: at
the bar *(au comptoir)*, sitting down *(la salle)*, and
outside *(la terrasse)*. Refills aren't free. Ask for the bill
when you're ready to leave. While a service charge is
included in the bill, it's polite to leave whatever small
coins are included in your change.

Wine:

In France, wine is not merely an agricultural product,
it's a work of art. Each wine-growing region and each
vintage has its own distinct personality. Burgundy and
Bordeaux are famous for their reds. The people of

Brittany are proud of their *Muscadet*. The Loire Valley produces the sweet white *Vouvray* wines. Lyon is known for its good-quality, low-priced *Côtes du Rhône*. And of course, the finest champagne in the world comes from... Champagne. As you explore France, look for the *dégustation* signs welcoming you in for a wine tasting. It's normally free or very cheap.

wine	**vin**	van
table wine	**vin de table**	van duh tah-bluh
cheap house wine	**vin ordinaire**	van or-dee-nair
local	**régional**	ray-zhee-oh-nahl
red	**rouge**	roozh
white	**blanc**	blahn
rose	**rosé**	roh-zay
sparkling	**mousseux**	moo-suh
sweet	**doux**	doo
medium	**demi-sec**	duh-mee sehk
dry	**sec**	sehk
very dry	**brut**	brewt
a glass...	**un verre...**	uhn vehr
a carafe...	**une carafe...**	ewn kah-rahf
...of red wine	**...de rouge**	duh roozh
...of white wine	**...de blanc**	duh blahn
a half bottle	**une demi-bouteille**	ewn duh-mee-boo-teh-ee
a bottle	**une bouteille**	ewn boo-teh-ee
The wine list.	**La carte des vins.**	lah kart day van

Beer:

beer	**bière**	bee-ehr
from the tap	**a là pression**	ah lah preh-see-oh<u>n</u>
light / dark	**blonde / brune**	blohnd / brewn
local	**régionale**	ray-zhee-oh-nahl
imported	**importée**	a<u>n</u>-por-tay
small beer /	**un demi /**	uh<u>n</u> duh-mee /
large beer	**une chope**	ewn shohp
alcohol-free	**sans alcool**	sah<u>n</u> zahl-kohl
cold	**froide**	frwahd

Bar talk:

What would you like?	**Qu'est-ce que vous prenez?**	kehs kuh voo pruh-nay
local specialty	**spécialité régionale**	spay-see-ah-lee-tay ray-zhee-oh-nahl
straight (dry)	**sec**	sehk
with / without...	**avec / sans...**	ah-vehk / sah<u>n</u>
...alcohol	**...alcool**	ahl-kohl
...ice	**...glaçons**	glah-soh<u>n</u>
One more.	**Encore une.**	ah<u>n</u>-kor ewn
Cheers!	**Santé!**	sah<u>n</u>-tay
To your health!	**À votre santé!**	ah voh-truh sah<u>n</u>-tay
Long live France!	**Vive la France!**	veev lah frah<u>n</u>s

I'm feeling...	**Je suis...**	zhuh swee
...a little drunk.	**...un peu ivre.**	uh<u>n</u> puh ee-vruh
...blitzed. (colloq.)	**...ivre mort.**	ee-vruh mor

Specialties *de la région* include many kinds of *eaux de vie* (fruit brandy), and *cassis* drinks (black currant liqueur) such as *kir* (cassis and white wine) and *kir royale* (cassis and champagne). *Pernod* is an anise-flavored *apéritif.*

Groceries and Picnics

Building your own meal:

market (open air)	**marché**	mar-shay
grocery store	**épicerie**	ay-pee-suh-ree
supermarket	**supermarché**	sew-pehr-mar-shay
super-duper market	**hypermarché**	ee-pehr-mar-shay
Is it self-service?	**C'est libre service?**	seh lee-bruh sehr-vees
picnic	**pique-nique**	peek neek
sandwich	**sandwich**	sahnd-weech
bread	**pain**	pan
whole wheat bread	**pain complet**	pan kohn-pleh
roll	**petit pain**	puh-tee pan
sausage	**saucisse**	soh-sees
ham	**jambon**	zhahn-bohn
cheese	**fromage**	froh-mahzh
a piece	**un morceau**	uhn mor-soh
a slice	**une tranche**	ewn trahnsh
sliced	**tranché**	trahn-shay
fifty grams	**cinquante grammes**	san-kahnt grahm
one hundred grams	**cent grammes**	sahn grahm
more / less	**plus / moins**	plew / mwan
yogurt	**yaourt**	yah-oort
plastic spoon	**cuillère en plastique**	kwee-yehr ahn plah-steek

paper plate	**assiette en papier**	ahs-yeht ah<u>n</u> pahp-yay
Can you make me a sandwich?	**Pouvez-vous me faire un sandwich?**	poo-vay-voo muh fair uh<u>n</u> sah<u>n</u>d-weech
To take out.	**Pour emporter.**	poor ah<u>n</u>-por-tay
Is there a park nearby?	**Il y a un parc près d'ici?**	ee lee ah uh<u>n</u> park preh dee-see
May we picnic here?	**Pouvons-nous pique-niquer ici?**	poo-voh<u>n</u>-noo peek-nee-kay ee-see
Enjoy your meal!	**Bon appétit!**	boh<u>n</u> ah-pay-tee

Part of the fun of traveling in France is visiting the various shops and bakeries to assemble a classy picnic. While you can opt for the one-stop *supermarchés*, it's more fun to practice your French while visiting the small shops. You can get bread at a *boulangerie*, meat at a *charcuterie* and cheese at a *fromagerie*. You can order meat and cheese by the gram. One hundred grams is about a quarter pound, enough for two sandwiches. For dessert, stop by a *pâtisserie*.

Sightseeing

Handy sightseeing questions:

Where is... / Where are...?	Où est... / Où sont...?	oo eh / oo sohn
...the best view	...la meilleure vue	lah meh-yur vew
...the main square	...la place principale	lah plahs pran-see-pahl
...the old town center	...la vieille ville	lah vee-eh-ee veel
...the museum	...le musée	luh mew-zay
...the castle	...le château	luh shah-toh
...the palace	...le palais	luh pah-leh
...the ruins	...les ruines	lay rween
...a festival	...une fête	ewn feht
...the tourist information office	...l'office du tourisme	loh-fees dew too-reez-muh
Do you have... in English?	Avez-vous... en anglais?	ah-vay-voo... ahn ahn-gleh
...information	...des renseignements	day rahn-sehn-yuh-mahn
...a guidebook	...une guide	ewn geed
...a tour	...une visite guidée	ewn vee-zeet gee-day
When is the next tour in English?	La prochaine visite en anglais sera à quelle heure?	lah proh-shehn vee-zeet ahn ahn-gleh suh-rah ah kehl ur
Is it free?	Est-ce gratuit?	ehs grah-twee
How much does it cost?	Combien?	kohn-bee-an

Is there a discount for...?	**Y a-t-il une réduction pour...?**	ee ah-teel ewn ray-dewk-see-ohn poor
...students	**...les étudiants**	lay zay-tew-dee-ahn
...seniors	**...les personnes âgée**	lay pehr-suhn ah-zhay
...youth	**...les jeunes gens**	lay zhuhn zhahn
Is the ticket good all day?	**Le billet est valable toute la journée?**	luh bee-yeh eh vah-lah-bluh toot lah zhoor-nay
What time does this open / close?	**Ça ouvre / ferme à quelle heure?**	sah oo-vruh / fehrm ah kehl ur
What time is the last entry?	**La dernière entrée est à quelle heure?**	lah dehrn-yehr ahn-tray eh tah kehl ur
PLEASE let me in.	**S'il vous plaît, laissez-moi entrer.**	see voo pleh leh-say-mwah ahn-tray
I've traveled all the way from...	**Je suis venu de...**	zhuh swee vuh-new duh
I must leave tomorrow.	**Il faut que je parte demain.**	eel foh kuh zhuh part duh-man

In France, national museums close on Tuesdays.

In the museum:

Where can I find this? (point to photo)	**Où puis-je trouver ça?**	oo pwee-zhuh troo-vay sah
I'd like to see...	**Je voudrais voir...**	zhuh voo-dreh vwahr
Are photos / videos allowed?	**Les photos / vidéos sont autorisées?**	lay foh-toh / vee-day-oh sohn toh-toh-ree-zay
No flash / tripod.	**Pas de flash / trépied.**	pah duh flahsh / tray-pee-yay

I like it.	Ça me plaît.	sah muh pleh
It's so...	C'est si...	seh see
...beautiful.	...beau.	boh
...ugly.	...laid.	leh
...strange.	...bizarre.	bee-zar
...boring.	...ennuyeux.	ahn-new-yuh
...interesting.	...intéressant.	an-tay-reh-sahn
Wow!	Sensass!	sahn-sahs
My feet hurt!	J'ai mal aux pieds!	zhay mahl oh pee-yay
I'm exhausted!	Je suis épuisé!	zhuh swee zay-pwee-zay

Art and architecture:

art	art	ar
artist	artiste	ar-teest
painting	tableau	tah-bloh
self-portrait	autoportrait	oh-toh-por-treh
sculptor	sculpteur	skewlp-tur
sculpture	sculpture	skewlp-tewr
architect	architecte	ar-shee-tehkt
architecture	architecture	ar-shee-tehk-tewr
original	original	oh-ree-zhee-nahl
restored	restauré	rehs-toh-ray
B.C.	av. J.-C.	ah-vahn zhay-zew-kree
A.D.	ap. J.-C.	ah-preh zhay-zew-kree
century	siècle	see-eh-kluh
style	style	steel
Abstract	abstrait	ahb-streh
Ancient	ancien	ahn-see-an
Art Nouveau	Art Nouveau	ar noo-voh
Baroque	baroque	bah-rohk

Classical	**classique**	klahs-seek
Gothic	**gothique**	goh-teek
Impressionist	**impressionniste**	an-preh-see-uh-neest
Medieval	**médiéval**	mayd-yay-vahl
Modern	**moderne**	moh-dehrn
Renaissance	**renaissance**	ruh-neh-sahns
Romanesque	**romanesque**	roh-mah-nehsk
Romantic	**romantique**	roh-mahn-teek

Castles and palaces:

castle	**château**	shah-toh
palace	**palais**	pah-leh
ballroom	**salle des fêtes**	sahl day feht
kitchen	**cuisine**	kwee-zeen
cellar	**cave**	kahv
dungeon	**donjon**	dohn-zhohn
fortified wall	**remparts**	rahn-par
tower	**tour**	toor
fountain	**fontaine**	fohn-tehn
garden	**jardin**	zhar-dan
king	**roi**	rwah
queen	**reine**	rehn
knights	**chevaliers**	shuh-vahl-yay

Religious words:

cathedral	**cathédrale**	kah-tay-drahl
church	**église**	ay-gleez
monastery	**monastère**	moh-nah-stehr
synagogue	**synagogue**	see-nah-gohg
chapel	**chapelle**	shah-pehl
altar	**autel**	oh-tehl
cross	**croix**	krwah
cloister	**cloître**	klwah-truh
crypt	**crypte**	kreept
dome	**dôme**	dohm
organ	**orgue**	org
relic	**relique**	ruh-leek
saint	**saint (m) / sainte (f)**	sah<u>n</u> / sah<u>n</u>t
God	**Dieu**	dee-uh
Jew	**juif**	zhweef
Christian	**chrétien**	kray-tee-a<u>n</u>
Protestant	**protestant**	proh-tehs-tah<u>n</u>
Catholic	**catholique**	kah-toh-leek
When is the service?	**La messe est à quelle heure?**	lah mehs eh tah kehl ur
Are there church concerts?	**Y a-t-il des concerts à l'église?**	ee ah-teel day koh<u>n</u>-sehr ah lay-gleez

Shopping

Names of French shops:

antiques	**antiquités**	ahn-tee-kee-tay
art gallery	**gallerie d'art**	gah-luh-ree dar
bakery	**boulangerie**	boo-lahn-zhuh-ree
barber shop	**coiffeur**	kwah-fur
beauty parlor	**coiffeur pour dames**	kwah-fur poor dahm
book shop	**librairie**	lee-breh-ree
camera shop	**boutique photographique**	boo-teek foh-toh-grah-feek
department store	**grand magasin**	grahn mah-gah-zan
flea market	**marché aux puces**	mar-shay oh pews
flower market	**marché aux fleurs**	mar-shay oh flur
grocery store	**épicerie**	ay-pee-suh-ree
jewelry shop	**bijouterie**	bee-zhoo-tuh-ree
laundromat	**laverie**	lah-vuh-ree
newsstand	**maison de la presse**	meh-zohn duh lah prehs
open air market	**marché en plein air**	mar-shay ahn plan air
pharmacy	**pharmacie**	far-mah-see
shopping mall	**centre commercial**	sahn-truh koh-mehr-see-ahl
souvenir shop	**boutique de souvenirs**	boo-teek duh soo-vuh-neer
supermarket	**supermarché**	sew-pehr-mar-shay
toy store	**magasin de jouets**	mah-gah-zan duh zhweh
travel agency	**agence de voyages**	ah-zhahns duh voy-yahzh

used bookstore	**boutique de livres d'occasion**	boo-teek duh lee-vruh doh-kah-zee-ohn
wine shop	**marchant de vin**	mar-shahn duh van

In France, most shops close for a long lunch (noon till about 14:00), and all day on Sundays and Mondays. Grocery stores are often open on Sunday mornings.

Shop till you drop:

sale	**solde**	sohld
How much does it cost?	**Combien?**	kohn-bee-an
I'd like...	**Je voudrais...**	zhuh voo-dreh
Do you have...?	**Avez-vous...?**	ah-vay-voo
...something cheaper	**...quelque chose de moins cher**	kehl-kuh shohz duh mwan shehr
Can I see more?	**Puis-je en voir d'autres?**	pweezh ahn vwahr doh-truh
This one.	**Celui-ci.**	suhl-wee-see
Can I try it on?	**Je peux l'essayer?**	zhuh puh leh-say-yay
A mirror?	**Un miroir?**	uhn meer-wahr
It's too big / small / expensive.	**C'est trop grand / petit / cher.**	seh troh grahn / puh-tee / shehr
Did you make this?	**C'est vous qui l'avez fait?**	seh voo kee lah-vay feh
What is it made out of?	**De quoi est-ce que c'est fait?**	duh kwah ehs kuh seh feh

English	French	Pronunciation
Machine washable?	**Lavable en machine?**	lah-vah-bluh ahn mah-sheen
Will it shrink?	**Ça va rétrécir?**	sah vah ray-tray-seer
Can you ship this?	**Pouvez-vous l'expédier?**	poo-vay voo lehk-spay-dee-ay
Can I pay with a credit card?	**Acceptez-vous les cartes de crédit?**	ahk-sehp-tay-voo lay kart duh kray-dee
Tax-free?	**Exempt de taxe?**	ehg-zahn duh tahks
I'll think about it.	**Je vais y penser.**	zhuh veh ee pahn-say
What time do you close?	**Vous fermez à quelle heure?**	voo fehr-may ah kehl ur
What time do you open tomorrow?	**À quelle heure allez-vous ouvrir demain?**	ah kehl ur ah-lay-voo zoo-vreer duh-man
Is that your lowest price?	**C'est votre prix le plus bas?**	seh voh-truh pree luh plew bah
My last offer.	**Ma dernière offre.**	mah dehrn-yehr oh-fruh
I'm nearly broke.	**Je suis presque fauché.**	zhuh swee prehsk foh-shay
No thanks, I'm just looking.	**Merci, je regarde.**	mehr-see zhuh ruh-gard
We're just grazing.	**Nous broutons.**	noo broo-tohn
My friend has the money.	**Mon ami a l'argent.**	mohn ah-mee ah lar-zhahn
My wife / my husband has the money.	**Ma femme / mon mari a l'argent.**	mah fahm / mohn mah-ree ah lar-zhahn

You can look up colors and fabrics in the *Rolling Rosetta Stone* Word Guide near the end of this book.

Mail

Licking the postal code:

Post, Telephone & Telegraph Office	**PTT**	pay tay tay
post office	**bureau de poste**	bew-roh duh pohst
stamp	**timbre**	ta<u>n</u>-bruh
post card	**carte postale**	kart poh-stahl
letter	**lettre**	leh-truh
aerogram	**aérogramme**	ay-roh-grahm
envelope	**enveloppe**	ah<u>n</u>-vuh-lohp
package	**colis**	koh-lee
box	**boîte en carton**	bwaht ah<u>n</u> kar-toh<u>n</u>
string / tape	**ficelle / bolduc**	fee-sehl / bohl-dewk
mailbox	**boîte aux lettres**	bwaht oh leh-truh
air mail	**par avion**	par ah-vee-oh<u>n</u>
express mail	**par express**	par ehk-sprehs
surface mail	**surface**	sewr-fahs
book rate	**tarif des livres**	tah-reef day lee-vruh
registered	**enregistré**	ah<u>n</u>-ruh-zhee-stray
insured	**assuré**	ah-sew-ray
fragile	**fragile**	frah-zheel
contents	**contenu**	koh<u>n</u>-tuh-new
customs	**douane**	doo-ahn

to / from	**à / de**	ah / duh
address	**adresse**	ah-drehs
zip code	**code postal**	kohd poh-stahl
general delivery	**poste restante**	pohst rehs-tah<u>nt</u>

Mail bonding:

Where is the PTT?	**Où est le PTT?**	oo eh luh pay tay tay
Which window for...?	**Quel guichet pour...?**	kehl gee-sheh poor
To the United States.	**Aux Etats-Unis.**	oh zay-tah-zew-nee
How much?	**Combien?**	koh<u>n</u>-bee-a<u>n</u>
How many... will it take?	**Ça va prendre combien de...?**	sah vah prahn-druh koh<u>n</u>-bee-a<u>n</u> duh
...days	**...jours**	zhoor
...weeks	**...semaines**	suh-mehn
...months	**...mois**	mwah

You can often get postage stamps at the corner *tabac* (tobacco shop). As long as you know which stamps you need, this is a great convenience.

Time

It's about time:

What time is it?	**Quelle heure est-il?**	kehl ur eh-teel
It's...	**Il est...**	eel eh
...8:00.	**...huit heures.**	weet ur
...13:30.	**...treize heures et demie.**	trehz ur ay duh-mee
...16:00.	**...seize heures.**	sehz ur
...a quarter past three.	**...trois heures et quart.**	trwahz ur ay kar
...a quarter to eleven.	**...onze heures moins le quart.**	ohnz ur mwan luh kar
...about 4:00 in the afternoon.	**...vers quatre heures de l'après-midi.**	vehr kah-truh ur duh lah-preh-mee-dee
...noon.	**...midi.**	mee-dee
...midnight.	**...minuit.**	mee-nwee
...too early.	**...trop tôt.**	troh toh
...too late.	**...trop tard.**	troh tar

Timely words:

minute	**minute**	mee-newt
hour	**heure**	ur
in one hour	**dans une heure**	dahn zewn ur
immediately	**immédiatement**	ee-may-dee-aht-mahn
any time	**n'importe quand**	nan-port kahn

every hour	**toutes les heures**	toot lay zur
every day	**tous les jours**	too lay zhoor
May 15	**le quinze mai**	luh kanz may

morning	**matin**	mah-tan
afternoon	**après-midi**	ah-preh-mee-dee
evening	**soir**	swahr
night	**nuit**	nwee
day	**jour**	zhoor
today	**aujourd'hui**	oh-zhoor-dwee
yesterday	**hier**	yehr
tomorrow	**demain**	duh-man
tomorrow morning	**demain matin**	duh-man mah-tan
week	**semaine**	suh-mehn
month	**mois**	mwah
year	**année**	ah-nay
last	**dernier**	dehrn-yay
this	**ce**	suh
next	**prochain**	proh-shan

Monday	**lundi**	luhn-dee
Tuesday	**mardi**	mar-dee
Wednesday	**mercredi**	mehr-kruh-dee
Thursday	**jeudi**	zhuh-dee
Friday	**vendredi**	vahn-druh-dee
Saturday	**samedi**	sahm-dee
Sunday	**dimanche**	dee-mahnsh

January	**janvier**	zhahn-vee-yay
February	**février**	fay-vree-yay
March	**mars**	mars
April	**avril**	ahv-reel
May	**mai**	may
June	**juin**	zhwan

July	**juillet**	zhwee-yeh
August	**août**	oot
September	**septembre**	sehp-tahn-bruh
October	**octobre**	ohk-toh-bruh
November	**novembre**	noh-vahn-bruh
December	**décembre**	day-sahn-bruh

spring	**printemps**	pran-tahn
summer	**été**	ay-tay
fall	**automne**	oh-tuhn
winter	**hiver**	ee-vehr
Ice Age	**période glaciaire**	pay-ree-ohd glah-see-air

French holidays:

holiday	**jour férié**	zhoor fay-ree-ay
national holiday	**fête nationale**	feht nah-see-oh-nahl
France's major holiday (July 14)	**le quatorze juillet**	luh kah-torz zhwee-yeh
religious holiday	**fête religieuse**	feht ruh-lee-zhuhz
Ascension of Mary (August 15)	**L'Ascension**	lah-sahn-see-ohn
Happy birthday!	**Bon anniversaire!**	bohn ah-nee-vehr-sair
Happy wedding anniversary!	**Bon anniversaire de mariage!**	bohn ah-nee-vehr-sair duh mah-ree-yahzh
Merry Christmas!	**Joyeux Noël!**	zhwah-yuh noh-ehl
Happy New Year!	**Bonne année!**	buhn ah-nay

July 14th is Bastille Day, the national holiday.
Festivities begin on the evening of the 13th and rage
throughout the country.

Red Tape and Profanity

Filling out forms:

Monsieur	Mr.
Madame / Mademoiselle	Mrs. / Miss
prénom	first name
nom	name
adresse	address
lieu de domicile	address
rue	street
ville	city
état	state
pays	country
nationalité	nationality
originaire de...	origin
destination	destination
âge	age
date de naissance	date of birth
lieu de naissance	place of birth
sexe	sex
mâle / femelle	male / female
marié / célibataire	married / single
profession	profession
adulte	adult
enfant / garçon / fille	child / boy / girl
enfants	children
famille	family
signature	signature

Handy / dangerous customs phrases:

customs	**douane**	doo-ahn
passport	**passeport**	pah-spor
Stamp it, please.	**Tamponez, s'il vous plaît.**	tahn-poh-nay see voo pleh
I am on vacation.	**Je suis en vacances.**	zhuh swee zahn vah-kahns
I have nothing to declare.	**Je n'ai rien à déclarer.**	zhuh nay ree-an ah day-klah-ray
I have no idea how that got there.	**Je n'ai aucune idée comment cela se trouve là.**	zhuh nay oh-kewn ee-day koh-mahn suh-lah suh troov lah
Was your father in the Gestapo?	**Votre père était dans le Gestapo?**	voh-truh pehr ay-teh dahn luh gehs-tah-poh
Nice doggie.	**Gentil petit toutou.**	zhahn-tee puh-tee too-too

French profanity:

Insulting a customs official is a serious offense. While you languish in prison, you'll hear some rough language.

Damn! (Good God!)	**Bon Dieu!**	bohn dee-uh
bastard	**salaud**	sah-loh
bitch	**salope**	sah-lohp
breasts (colloq.)	**tétons**	tay-tohn
big breasts	**grands tétons**	grahn tay-tohn
penis (colloq.)	**bite**	beet
butthole	**sale con**	sahl kohn
shit	**merde**	mehrd
drunk	**bourré**	boo-ray
idiot	**idiot**	ee-dee-oh
imbecile	**imbécile**	an-bay-seel
jerk	**connard**	kuh-nar
stupid	**stupide**	stew-peed
Did someone...?	**Est-ce que quelqu'un à...?**	ehs kuh kehl-kuhn ah
...burp	**...roter**	roh-tay
...fart	**...péter**	pay-tay

Health

Handy health words:

pain	**douleur**	doo-lur
dentist	**dentiste**	dahn-teest
doctor	**docteur**	dohk-tur
nurse	**garde-malade**	gard-mah-lahd
health insurance	**assurance**	ah-sew-rahns
	maladie	mah-lah-dee
hospital	**hôpital**	oh-pee-tahl
medicine	**médicaments**	may-dee-kah-mahn
pharmacy	**pharmacie**	far-mah-see
prescription	**ordonnance**	or-duh-nahns
pill	**pilule**	pee-lewl
aspirin	**aspirine**	ah-spee-reen
antibiotic	**antibiotique**	ahn-tee-bee-oh-teek
pain killer	**calmant**	kahl-mahn
bandage	**bandage**	bahn-dahzh

Finding a cure:

I feel sick.	**Je me sens malade.**	zhuh muh sahn mah-lahd
I need a doctor...	**Il me faut un**	eel muh foh uhn
	docteur...	dohk-tur
...who speaks English.	**...qui parle anglais.**	kee parl ahn-gleh

It hurts here.	**Ça me fait mal ici.**	sah muh feh mahl ee-see
I'm allergic to...	**Je suis allergique à...**	zhuh swee zah-lehr-zheek ah
...penicillin.	**...pénicilline.**	pay-nee-see-leen
I am diabetic.	**Je suis diabétique.**	zhuh swee dee-ah-bay-teek
This is serious.	**C'est sérieux.**	seh say-ree-uh
I have...	**J'ai...**	zhay
...a burn.	**...une brûlure.**	ewn brew-lewr
...chest pains.	**...mal à la poitrine.**	mahl ah lah pwah-treen
...a cold.	**...un rhume.**	uhn rewm
...constipation.	**...la constipation.**	lah kohn-stee-pah-see-ohn
...a cough.	**...une toux.**	ewn too
...diarrhea.	**...la diarrhée.**	lah dee-ah-ray
...a fever.	**...une fièvre.**	ewn fee-eh-vruh
...the flu.	**...la grippe.**	lah greep
...a headache.	**...mal à la tête.**	mahl ah lah teht
...indigestion.	**...une indigestion.**	ewn an-dee-zheh-stee-ohn
...an infection.	**...une infection.**	ewn an-fehk-see-ohn
...nausea.	**...la nausée.**	lah noh-zay
...a rash.	**...des boutons.**	day boo-tohn
...a sore throat.	**...mal à la gorge.**	mahl ah lah gorzh
...a stomach ache.	**...mal à l'estomac.**	mahl ah luh-stoh-mah
...a swelling.	**...une enflure.**	ewn ahn-flewr
...a toothache.	**...mal aux dents.**	mahl oh dahn
...a venereal disease.	**...une maladie vénérienne.**	ewn mah-lah-dee vay-nay-ree-ehn

...worms.	**...des vers.**	day vehr
I have body odor.	**Je sens mauvais.**	zhuh sahn moh-veh
Is it serious?	**C'est sérieux?**	seh say-ree-uh

Contact lenses:

hard lenses	**verres de contact durs**	vehr duh kohn-tahkt dewr
soft lenses	**verres de contact mous**	vehr duh kohn-tahkt moo
cleaning solution	**solution nettoyage**	soh-lew-see-ohn neh-toy-yahzh
soaking solution	**solution à trempage**	soh-lew-see-ohn ah trahn-pahzh
I've... a contact lens.	**J'ai... un de mes verres de contact.**	zhay... uhn duh may vehr duh kohn-tahkt
...lost	**...perdu**	pehr-dew
...swallowed	**...avalé**	ah-vah-lay

Help!

Help in general:

Help!	**Au secours!**	oh suh-koor
Help me!	**A l'aide!**	ah lehd
Call a doctor!	**Appelez un docteur!**	ah-play uhn dohk-tur
ambulance	**ambulance**	ahn-bew-lahns
accident	**accident**	ahk-see-dahn
injured	**blessé**	bleh-say
emergency	**urgence**	ewr-zhahns
police	**police**	poh-lees
thief	**voleur**	voh-lur
pick-pocket	**pickpocket**	peek-poh-keht
I've been ripped off.	**On m'a volé.**	ohn mah voh-lay
I've lost...	**J'ai perdu...**	zhay pehr-dew
...my passport.	**...mon passeport.**	mohn pah-spor
...my ticket.	**...mon billet.**	mohn bee-yeh
...my baggage.	**...mes bagages.**	may bah-gahzh
...my purse.	**...mon sac.**	mohn sahk
...my wallet.	**...mon portefeuille.**	mohn por-tuh-fuh-ee
...my faith in humankind.	**...ma foi en l'humanité.**	mah fwah ahn lew-mah-nee-tay
I'm lost.	**Je suis perdu.**	zhuh swee pehr-dew

Help for women:

Leave me alone.	**Laissez-moi tranquille.**	leh-say-mwah trahn-keel
I wish to be alone.	**Je préfère être seule.**	zhuh pray-fehr eh-truh suhl
I'm not interested.	**Ça ne m'intéresse pas.**	sah nuh man-tay-rehs pah
I'm married.	**Je suis mariée.**	zhuh swee mah-ree-ay
I'm a lesbian.	**Je suis lesbienne.**	zhuh swee lehz-bee-ehn
I have a contagious disease.	**J'ai une maladie contagieuse.**	zhay ewn mah-lah-dee kohn-tah-zhuhz
Stop following me.	**Arrêtez de me suivre.**	ah-reh-tay duh muh swee-vruh
Don't touch me.	**Ne me touchez pas.**	nuh muh too-shay pah
Enough!	**Ça suffit!**	sah sew-fee
Get lost!	**Dégagez!**	day-gah-zhay
Drop dead!	**Allez vous faire voir!**	ah-lay voo fair vwahr
I'll call the police.	**J'appelle la police.**	zhah-pehl lah poh-lees
Police!	**Police!**	poh-lees

Conversations

Getting to know you:

My name is...	**Je m'appelle...**	zhuh mah-pehl
What's your name?	**Comment vous appelez-vous?**	koh-mahn voo zah-play-voo
How are you?	**Comment allez-vous?**	koh-mahn tah-lay-voo
I am... / You are...	**Je suis... / Vous êtes...**	zhuh swee / voo zeht
...fine.	**...bien.**	bee-an
...tired.	**...fatigué.**	fah-tee-gay
...sad.	**...triste.**	treest
...happy.	**...content (m) / contente (f).**	kohn-tahn / kohn-tahnt
I am... / You are...	**J'ai... / Vous avez...**	zhay / voo zah-vay
...hungry.	**...faim.**	fan
...thirsty.	**...soif.**	swahf
...cold.	**...froid.**	frwah
...lucky.	**...de la chance.**	duh lah shahns
I don't smoke.	**Je ne fume pas.**	zhuh nuh fewm pah
Where are you from?	**D'où venez-vous?**	doo vuh-nay-voo
What city?	**Quelle ville?**	kehl veel
What country?	**Quel pays?**	kehl peh-ee
What planet?	**Quelle planète?**	kehl plah-neht

I'm an American.	**Je suis américain (m) / américaine (f).**	zhuh sweez ah-may-ree-kan / ah-may-ree-kehn
This is my friend.	**C'est mon ami.**	seh mohn ah-mee
This is...	**C'est...**	seh
... my boy friend / my girl friend.	**...mon petit ami / ma petite amie.**	mohn puh-tee tah-mee / mah puh-tee tah-mee
...my husband / my wife.	**...mon mari / ma femme.**	mohn mah-ree / mah fahm
...my son / my daughter.	**...mon fils / ma fille.**	mohn fees / mah fee-ee
...my brother / my sister.	**...mon frère / ma soeur.**	mohn frehr / mah sur
...my father / my mother.	**...mon père / ma mère.**	mohn pehr / mah mehr

Family, school and work:

Are you married?	**Êtes-vous marié?**	eht voo mah-ree-ay
Do you have children?	**Avez-vous des enfants?**	ah-vay-voo day zahn-fahn
Do you have photos?	**Avez-vous des photos?**	ah-vay voo day foh-toh
How old is your child?	**Quel âge à votre enfant?**	kehl ahzh ah voh-truh ahn-fahn
Beautiful child / beautiful children!	**Bel enfant / beaux enfants!**	behl ahn-fahn / boh zahn-fahn
Beautiful boy / beautiful girl!	**Beau garçon / belle fille!**	boh gar-sohn / behl fee-ee

What are you studying?	**Qu'est-ce que vous étudiez?**	kehs kuh voo zay-tew-dee-ay
How old are you?	**Quel âge avez-vous?**	kehl ahzh ah-vay-voo
I'm... years old.	**J'ai... ans.**	zhay... ah<u>n</u>
Do you have brothers and sisters?	**Avez-vous des frères et soeurs?**	ah-vay-voo day frehr ay sur
What is your occupation?	**Quelle est votre occupation?**	kehl eh voh-truh oh-kew-pah-see-oh<u>n</u>
I'm a...	**Je suis...**	zhuh swee
...student.	**...étudiant (m) / étudiante (f).**	zay-tew-dee-ah<u>n</u> / zay-tew-dee-ah<u>n</u>t
...teacher.	**...professeur.**	proh-feh-sur
...worker.	**...ouvrier.**	oo-vree-ay
...brain surgeon.	**...chirurgien cérébral.**	shee-rewr-zhee-a<u>n</u> say-ray-brahl
...professional traveler.	**...voyageur professionel.**	voy-yah-zhur proh-feh-see-oh-nehl
Do you like your work?	**Aimez-vous votre occupation?**	eh-may-voo voh-truh oh-kew-pah-see-oh<u>n</u>

Travel talk:

Are you on vacation?	**Êtes-vous en vacances?**	eht-voo zah<u>n</u> vah-kah<u>n</u>s
A business trip?	**Un voyage d'affaires?**	uh<u>n</u> voy-yahzh dah-fair

How long have you been traveling?	**Il y a longtemps que vous voyagez?**	ee lee yah lohn-tahn kuh voo voy-yah-zhay
day / week	**jour / semaine**	zhoor / suh-mehn
month / year	**mois / année**	mwah / ah-nay
When are you going home?	**Quand allez-vous rentrer?**	kahn ah-lay-voo rahn-tray
This is my first time in...	**C'est la première fois que je visite...**	seh lah pruhm-yehr fwah kuh zhuh vee-zeet
I've visited... and then...	**J'ai visité... et puis...**	zhay vee-zee-tay... ay pwee
Today / tomorrow I go to...	**Aujourd'hui / demain je vais à...**	oh-zhoor-dwee / duh-man zhuh veh ah
I'm homesick.	**J'ai le mal du pays.**	zhay luh mahl dew peh-ee
I'm very happy here.	**Je suis content (m) / contente (f) ici.**	zhuh swee kohn-tahn / kohn-tahnt ee-see
The French are very friendly.	**Les Français sont très gentils.**	lay frahn-say sohn treh zhahn-tee
France is a wonderful country.	**La France est un pays magnifique.**	lah frahns eh tuhn peh-ee mahn-yee-feek
To travel is to live.	**Voyager c'est vivre.**	voy-yah-zhay seh vee-vruh

Weather:

What's the weather tomorrow?	**Quel temps fera-t-il demain?**	kehl tahn fuh-rah-teel duh-man
sunny / rainy	**ensoleillé / pluvieux**	ahn-soh-leh-yay / pluh-vee-uh
hot / cold	**chaud / froid**	shoh / frwah

Favorite things:

What kind...	**Quelle sorte...**	kehl sort...
do you like?	**aimez-vous?**	eh-may-voo
...of art	**...d'art**	dar
...of books	**...de livres**	duh lee-vruh
...of hobby	**...de hobby**	duh oh-bee
...of ice cream	**...de glace**	duh glahs
...of movies	**...de films**	duh feelm
...of music	**...de musique**	duh mew-zeek
...of sports	**...de sports**	duh spor
...of vices	**...de vices**	duh vees
Who is your...?	**Qui est votre...?**	kee eh voh-truh
...favorite male singer	**...chanteur favorit**	shahn-tur fah-voh-ree
...favorite female singer	**...chanteuse favorite**	shahn-tuhz fah-voh-reet
...favorite movie star	**...vedette favorite**	vuh-deht fah-voh-reet

Responses for all occasions:

I like that.	**Ça me plaît.**	sah muh pleh
I like you.	**Je t'aime bien.**	zhuh tehm bee-an
That's cool.	**C'est chouette.**	seh shweht
Great!	**Formidable!**	for-mee-dah-bluh
Perfect.	**Parfait.**	par-feh
Funny.	**Amusant.**	ah-mew-zahn
Very interesting.	**Très intéressant.**	treh zan-tay-reh-sahn
Really?	**Vraiment?**	vreh-mahn

Congratulations!	**Félicitations!**	fay-lee-see-tah-see-oh<u>n</u>
You're welcome.	**Je vous en prie.**	zhuh voo zah<u>n</u> pree
Bless you! (after sneeze)	**À vos souhaits!**	ah voh sweh
What a pity.	**Quel dommage.**	kehl doh-mahzh
No problem.	**Pas de problème.**	pahd proh-blehm
OK.	**D'accord.**	dah-kor
That's life.	**C'est la vie.**	seh lah vee
This is the good life!	**Que la vie est belle!**	kuh lah vee eh behl
Have a good trip!	**Bon voyage!**	boh<u>n</u> voy-yahzh
Good luck!	**Bonne chance!**	buhn shah<u>n</u>s
Let's go!	**Allons-y!**	ah-loh<u>n</u>-zee

Thanks a million:

You are...	**Vous êtes...**	voo zeht
...kind.	**...gentil.**	zhah<u>n</u>-tee
...wonderful.	**...magnifique.**	mahn-yee-feek
...helpful.	**...obligeant.**	oh-blee-zhah<u>n</u>
...generous.	**...genereux.**	zhuh-nuh-ruh
...hairy.	**...velu.**	vuh-lew
This is / This was great fun.	**C'est / C'était bien amusant.**	seh / say-teh bee-a<u>n</u> ah-mew-zah<u>n</u>
You've gone to much trouble.	**Vous avez trop fait pour moi.**	voo zah-vay troh feh poor mwah
You are an angel from God.	**Vous êtes un ange de Dieu.**	voo zeht uh<u>n</u> ah<u>n</u>zh duh dee-uh

I will remember you...	**Je me souviendrai...**	zhuh muh soov-yan-dreh
...always.	**...toujours.**	too-zhoor
...till Tuesday.	**...à mardi.**	ah mar-dee

Conversing with French animals:

rooster / cock-a-doodle-doo	**coq / cocorico**	kohk / koh-koh-ree-koh
bird / tweet tweet	**oiseau / cui cui**	wah-zoh / kwee kwee
cat / meow	**chat / miaou**	shah / mee-ah-oo
dog / woof woof	**chien / ouah ouah**	shee-an / wah wah
duck / quack quack	**canard / coin coin**	kah-nar / kwan kwan
cow / moo	**vache / meu**	vahsh / muh
pig / oink oink	**cochon / groin groin**	koh-shohn / grwan grwan

Politics and Philosophy

The French enjoy deep conversations. With these lists, you can build sentences that will sound either deep or ridiculous, depending on your mood (and theirs).

Who:

politicians	**les politiciens**	lay poh-lee-tee-see-a<u>n</u>
big business	**les grosses affaires**	lay grohs ah-fair
mafia	**la mafia**	lah mah-fee-ah
military	**le militaire**	luh mee-lee-tair
the system	**le système**	luh sees-tehm
the rich	**les riches**	lay reesh
the poor	**les pauvres**	lay poh-vruh
men	**les hommes**	lay ohm
women	**les femmes**	lay fehm
children	**les enfants**	lay zah<u>n</u>-fah<u>n</u>
the French	**les Francais**	lay frah<u>n</u>-seh
the Americans	**les Américains**	lay zah-may-ree-ka<u>n</u>
the Germans	**les Allemands**	lay zahl-mah<u>n</u>
the Italians	**les Italiens**	lay zee-tah-lee-a<u>n</u>
I / you	**je / vous**	zhuh / voo
everyone	**tout le monde**	too luh moh<u>n</u>d

What:

want	**vouloir**	vool-wahr
need	**avoir besoln de**	ahv-wahr buh-swa<u>n</u> duh
take	**prendre**	prah<u>n</u>-druh
give	**donner**	duh-nay

prosper	**prospérer**	proh-spay-ray
suffer	**souffrir**	soo-freer
love	**aimer**	eh-may
hate	**détester**	day-teh-stay
work	**travailler**	trah-vah-yay
play	**jouer**	zhoo-way
vote	**voter**	voh-tay

Why:

love	**amour**	ah-moor
sex	**sexe**	"sex"
money	**argent**	ar-zhahn
power	**pouvoir**	poov-wahr
family	**famille**	fah-mee-ee
work	**travail**	trah-vah-ee
food	**nourriture**	noo-ree-tewr
health	**santé**	sahn-tay
hope	**espoir**	ehs-pwahr
religion	**religion**	ruh-lee-zhee-ohn
happiness	**bonheur**	bohn-ur
war / peace	**guerre / paix**	gehr / peh
democracy	**démocratie**	day-moh-krah-see
taxes	**taxes**	tahx
lies	**mensonges**	mahn-sohnzh
corruption	**corruption**	koh-rewp-see-ohn
pollution	**pollution**	poh-lew-see-ohn
recreational drugs	**drogues**	drohg
	récréatives	ray-kray-ah-teev

You be the judge:

(not) important	**(pas) important**	(pah) an-por-tahn
(not) powerful	**(pas) fort**	(pah) for
(not) honest	**(pas) honnête**	(pah) uh-neht
(not) innocent	**(pas) innocent**	(pah) een-noh-sahn
(not) greedy	**(pas) avide**	(pas) ah-veed
liberal	**libéral**	lee-bay-rahl
conservative	**conservateur**	kohn-sehr-vah-tur
radical	**radical**	rah-dee-kahl
too much	**trop**	troh
enough	**assez**	ah-say
never enough	**jamais assez**	jah-meh ah-say
worse / same /	**pire / même /**	peer / mehm /
better	**mieux**	mee-uh
good / bad	**bon / mauvais**	bohn / moh-veh
here / everywhere	**ici / partout**	ee-see / par-too

Assorted beginnings and endings:

I like... / I don't like...	**J'aime... /**	zhehm /
	Je n'aime pas...	zhuh nehm pah
Do you like...?	**Aimez-vous...?**	eh-may-voo
I am... / Are you...?	**Je suis... /**	zhuh swee /
	Êtes-vous...?	eht-voo
I believe... /	**Je crois... /**	zhuh krwah /
I don't believe...	**Je ne crois pas...**	zhuh nuh krwah pah
Do you believe...?	**Croyez-vous...?**	krwah-yay-voo
...in God	**...en Dieu**	ahn dee-uh
...in reincarnation	**...à la réin-**	ah lah ray-an-
	carnation	kar-nah-see-ohn

...in extraterrestrial life	**...dans la vie extraterrestre**	dahn lah vee ehk-strah-tuh-rehs-truh
...in Clinton	**...en Clinton**	ahn "Clinton"
Yes. / No.	**Oui. / Non.**	wee / nohn
Maybe. / I don't know.	**Peut-être. / Je ne sais pas.**	puh-teh-truh / zhuh nuh seh pah
What's most important in life?	**Quel est le plus important dans la vie?**	kehl eh luh plew zan-por-tahn dahn lah vee
The problem is...	**Le problème, c'est que...**	luh proh-blehm seh kuh
The answer is...	**La solution, c'est...**	luh soh-lew-see-ohn seh
We have solved the world's problems.	**Nous avons résolu les problèmes du monde.**	noo zah-vohn ray-zoh-lew lay proh-blehm dew mohnd

Entertainment

What's happening:

movie	**film**	feelm
...original version	**...version originale (V.O.)**	vehr-see-oh<u>n</u> oh-ree-zhee-nahl
...in English	**...en anglais**	ah<u>n</u> ah<u>n</u>-gleh
...with subtitles	**...avec sous-titres**	ah-vehk soo-tee-truh
...dubbed	**...doublé**	doo-blay
music	**musique**	mew-zeek
...classical	**...classique**	klahs-seek
...folk	**...folklorique**	fohk-loh-reek
...live	**...en directe**	ah<u>n</u> dee-rehkt
old rock	**rock classique**	rohk klahs-seek
jazz	**jazz**	zhazz
blues	**blues**	"blues"
singer	**chanteur (m) / chanteuse (f)**	shahn-tur / shah<u>n</u>-tuhz
concert	**concert**	koh<u>n</u>-sehr
show	**spectacle**	spehk-tahk-luh
sound and light show	**son et lumière**	soh<u>n</u> ay lew-mee-ehr
dancing	**danse**	dah<u>n</u>s
folk dancing	**danse folklorique**	dah<u>n</u>s fohk-loh-reek
disco	**disco**	dee-skoh
cover charge	**couvert**	koo-vehr

A night on the town:

English	French	Pronunciation
Can you recommend...?	**Pouvez-vous suggerer...?**	poo-vay-voo sewg-zhuh-ray
What's happening tonight?	**Qu'est-ce qui ce passe ce soir?**	kehs kee suh pahs suh swahr
Where can I buy a ticket?	**Où puis-je acheter un billet?**	oo pwee-zhuh ah-shuh-tay uhn bee-yeh
When does it start?	**Ça commence à quelle heure?**	sah koh-mahns ah kehl ur
When does it end?	**Ça se termine à quelle heure?**	sah suh tehr-meen ah kehl ur
The best place to dance nearby?	**Le meilleur dancing dans le coin?**	luh meh-yur dahn-seeng dahn luh kwan
Do you want to dance?	**Voulez-vous danser?**	voo-lay-voo dahn-say
Again?	**De nouveau?**	duh noo-voh
Let's paint the town red.	**Faisons la bringue.**	feh-zohn lah bran-guh
Let's have fun like idiots.	**Amusons-nous comme des fous.**	ah-mew-zohn-noo kohm day foo

A French Romance

Ah, l'amour:

What's the matter?	**Qu'est-ce qu'il y a?**	kehs kee lee yah
Nothing.	**Rien.**	ree-an
I / me / you	**je / moi / vous**	zhuh / mwah / voo
flirt (v)	**flirter**	fleer-tay
kiss (v)	**embrasser**	ahn-brah-say
hug (v)	**étreindre**	ay-tran-druh
love (n)	**amour**	ah-moor
make love	**faire l'amour**	fair lah-moor
condom	**préservatif**	pray-zehr-vah-teef
contraceptive	**contraceptif**	kohn-trah-sehp-teef
safe sex	**safe sex**	"safe sex"
sexy	**sexy**	"sexy"
cozy	**douillet**	doo-yeh
romantic	**romantique**	roh-mahn-teek
my angel	**mon ange**	mohn ahnzh
my doe	**ma biche**	mah beesh
my pussy cat	**mon chat**	mohn shah
my little cabbage	**mon petit chou**	mohn puh-tee shoo

I am...	**Je suis...**	zhuh swee
...gay.	**...homosexuel.**	oh-moh-sehk-sew-ehl
...straight.	**...hétéro.**	ay-tay-roh
...undecided.	**...indécis.**	an-day-see
...prudish.	**...pudibond (m) / pudibonde (f).**	pew-dee-bohn / pew-dee-bohnd
...horney.	**...excité.**	ehk-see-tay
We are on our honeymoon.	**C'est notre lune de miel.**	seh noh-truh lewn duh mee-ehl
I have...	**J'ai...**	zhay
...a boy friend.	**...un petit ami.**	uhn puh-tee tah-mee
...a girl friend.	**...une petite amie.**	ewn puh-tee tah-mee
I am married / I am not married.	**Je suis marié / Je ne suis pas marié.**	zhuh swee mah-ree-ay / zhuh nuh swee pah mah-ree-ay
I am rich and single.	**Je suis riche et célibataire.**	zhuh swee reesh ay say-lee-bah-tair
I am lonely.	**Je m'ennuie.**	zhuh mahn-nwee
I have no diseases.	**Je n'ai pas de maladies.**	zhuh nay pah duh mah-lah-dee
I have many diseases.	**J'ai plusieurs maladies.**	zhay plewz-yur mah-lah-dee
Can I see you again?	**On peut se revoir?**	ohn puh suh ruh-vwahr
You are my most beautiful souvenir.	**Vous êtes mon plus beau souvenir.**	voo zeht mohn plew boh soo-vuh-neer
Is this an aphrodisiac?	**C'est un aphrodisiaque?**	seh tuhn ah-froh-dee-zee-yahk
This is my first time.	**C'est la première fois.**	seh lah pruhm-yehr fwah

This is not my first time.	**Ce n'est pas la première fois.**	seh neh pah lah pruhm-yehr fwah
Do you do this often?	**Vous le faites souvent?**	voo luh feht soo-vahn
How's my breath?	**Comment trouvez-vous mon haleine?**	koh-mahn troo-vay-voo mohn ah-lehn
Let's just be friends.	**Soyons amis.**	swah-yohn zah-mee
I'll pay for my share.	**Je paie mon écot.**	zhuh peh mohn ay-koh
Would you like a massage...?	**Voulez-vous un massage...?**	voo-lay-voo uhn mah-sahzh
...for your feet	**...des pieds**	day pee-yay
Why not?	**Pourquoi pas?**	poor-kwah pah
Try it.	**Essayez-le.**	eh-say-yay-luh
That tickles.	**Ça chatouille.**	sah shah-too-ee
Oh my God.	**Mon Dieu.**	mohn dee-uh
I love you.	**Je t'aime.**	zhuh tehm
Darling, will you marry me?	**Chéri, veux-tu m'épouser?**	shay-ree vuh-tew may-poo-zay

The Rolling Rosetta Stone Word Guide

For centuries, Egyptian hieroglyphics were considered undecipherable -- until 1799, when a black slab known as the Rosetta Stone was unearthed in the Egyptian desert. By repeating identical phrases in hieroglyphics, Greek, and a newer form of Egyptian, Rosetta helped scientists break the ancient hieroglyphic code, and thus she became the grandmother of all phrasebooks.

As you roll through France, our thoroughly modern, portable Rosetta will help you translate key English words into French. These are in English alphabetical order, from left to right.

English	French	English	French
A		**A**	
above	**au dessus**	accident	**accident**
adaptor	**adapteur**	address	**adresse**
adult	**adulte**	afraid	**peur**
after	**après**	afternoon	**après-midi**
aftershave	**après rasage**	afterwards	**après**
again	**encore**	age	**âge**
agency	**agence**	aggressive	**aggressif**
agree	**d'accord**	AIDS	**SIDA**
air	**l'air**	air-conditioned	**climatisé**
airline	**ligne aérienne**	air mail	**par avion**
airport	**aéroport**	alarm clock	**réveille-matin**
alcohol	**alcool**	allergic	**allergique**
allergies	**allergies**	all together	**tous**
			ensemble
alone	**seule**	always	**toujours**

English	French	English	French
am (to be)	**suis (être)**	ancestor	**ancêtre**
ancient	**ancien**	and	**et**
angry	**fâché**	animal	**animal**
another	**encore**	answer	**réponse**
antibiotic	**antibiotique**	antiques	**antiquités**
apartment	**appartement**	apology	**excuses**
appetizers	**hors-d'oeuvre**	apple	**pomme**
appointment	**rendez-vous**	approximately	**presque**
area	**région**	arrest	**arrêter**
arrivals	**arrivées**	art	**l'art**
artificial	**artificial**	artist	**artiste**
ask	**demander**	aspirin	**aspirine**
at	**à**	Austria	**Autriche**
autumn	**automne**		

B   ## B

English	French	English	French
baby	**bébé**	babysitter	**babysitter**
backpack	**sac à dos**	bad	**mauvais**
baggage	**bagages**	bakery	**boulangerie**
balcony	**balcon**	ball	**balle**
banana	**banane**	Band-Aid	**bandage adhésif**
bank	**banque**	barber	**coiffeur**
basement	**sous-sol**	basket	**pannier**
bath	**bain**	bathroom	**salle de bains**
bathtub	**bain**	battery	**batterie**
beach	**plage**	beard	**barbe**
beautiful	**belle**	because	**parce que**
bed	**lit**	bedroom	**chambre**
bed sheet	**draps**	beef	**boeuf**

English	French	English	French
beer	**bière**	before	**avant**
begin	**commencer**	behind	**derrière**
below	**sous**	belt	**ceinture**
best	**le meilleur**	better	**meilleur**
bicycle	**vélo**	big	**grand**
bill (payment)	**addition**	bird	**oiseau**
birthday	**anniversaire**	black	**noir**
blanket	**couverture**	bleed	**saigner**
blond	**blonde**	blood	**sang**
blue	**bleu**	boat	**bateau**
body	**corps**	boil (v)	**bouillir**
boiling	**bouillant**	bomb	**bombe**
book	**livre**	book shop	**librairie**
boots	**bottes**	border	**frontière**
borrow	**emprunter**	boss	**chef**
bottle	**bouteille**	bottom	**fond**
bowl	**bol**	box	**boîte**
boy	**garçon**	bra	**soutien-gorge**
bread	**pain**	breakfast	**petit déjeuner**
bridge	**pont**	briefs	**slip**
Britain	**Grande-Bretagne**	broken	**en panne**
brother	**frère**	brown	**brun**
browsing	**regarder**	bucket	**seau**
building	**bâtiment**	bulb	**ampoule**
burn (n)	**brûlure**	bus	**bus**
business	**affaires**	button	**bouton**
by (via)	**en**		

English	French	English	French

C

C

English	French	English	French
calendar	**calendrier**	calorie	**calorie**
camera	**appareil-photo**	camping	**camping**
can (v)	**pouvoir**	can opener	**ouvre-boîte**
canal	**canal**	candle	**chandelle**
candy	**bonbon**	canoe	**canoë**
cap	**casquette**	captain	**capitaine**
car	**voiture**	carafe	**carafe**
card	**carte**	cards (deck)	**jeu de cartes**
careful	**prudent**	carpet	**moquette**
carrots	**carottes**	carry	**porter**
cashier	**caisse**	cassette	**cassette**
castle	**château**	cat	**chat**
catch (v)	**attraper**	cathedral	**cathédrale**
cave	**grotte**	cellar	**cave**
center	**centre**	century	**siècle**
chair	**chaise**	change (n)	**change**
cheap	**bon marché**	check	**chèque**
Cheers!	**Santé!**	cheese	**fromage**
chicken	**poulet**	children	**enfants**
chin	**menton**	Chinese (adj)	**chinois**
chocolate	**chocolat**	Christmas	**Noël**
church	**église**	cinema	**cinéma**
city	**ville**	city hall	**mairie**
class	**classe**	clean (adj)	**propre**
clear	**clair**	cliff	**falaise**
closed	**fermé**	clothesline	**corde à linge**
clothes pins	**pince à linge**	cloudy	**nuageux**
coast	**côte**	coffee	**café**
coins	**pièces**	cold (adj)	**froid**

English	French	English	French
colors	**couleurs**	comb (n)	**peigne**
come	**venir**	comfortable	**confortable**
complain	**se plaindre**	complicated	**compliqué**
computer	**ordinateur**	concert	**concert**
condom	**préservatif**	conductor	**conducteur**
congratulations	**félicitations**	connection (train)	**correspondance**
constipation	**constipation**	cook (v)	**cuisinier**
cool	**frais**	cork	**bouchon**
corkscrew	**tire-bouchon**	corner	**coin**
corridor	**couloir**	cost (v)	**coûter**
cot	**lit de camp**	cotton	**coton**
cough (v)	**tousser**	cough drops	**pastilles**
country	**pays**	countryside	**compagne**
cousin	**cousin**	cow	**vâche**
crafts	**arts**	cream	**crème**
credit card	**carte de crédit**	crowd (n)	**foule**
cry (v)	**pleurer**	cup	**tasse**

D

D

English	French	English	French
dad	**papa**	dance (v)	**danser**
danger	**danger**	dangerous	**dangereux**
dark	**sombre**	daughter	**fille**
day	**jour**	dead	**mort**
dear	**chéri**	delay	**retardement**
delicious	**délicieux**	dental floss	**fil dentaire**
dentist	**dentiste**	deodorant	**désodorisant**
departures	**départs**	deposit	**dépôt**
dessert	**dessert**	detour	**déviation**
diabetic	**diabétique**	diamond	**diamant**

English	French	English	French
diarrhea	**diarrhée**	dictionary	**dictionnaire**
difficult	**difficile**	dinner	**dîner**
direct	**direct**	direction	**direction**
dirty	**sale**	discount	**réduction**
disease	**maladie**	disturb	**déranger**
divorced	**divorcé**	doctor	**docteur**
document	**document**	dog	**chien**
doll	**poupée**	donkey	**âne**
door	**porte**	dormitory	**dortoire**
double	**double**	down	**en bas**
dream (n)	**rêve**	dress (n)	**robe**
drink (n)	**boisson**	drive (v)	**conduire**
driver	**chauffeur**	drunk	**ivre**
dry	**sec**		

E

E

English	French	English	French
each	**chaque**	ear	**oreille**
early	**tôt**	earplugs	**boules quiès**
earrings	**boucle d'oreille**	earth	**terre**
east	**est**	Easter	**Pâques**
easy	**facile**	eat	**manger**
elbow	**coude**	elevator	**ascenseur**
embarrassing	**gênant**	embassy	**ambassade**
empty	**vide**	English	**anglais**
enough	**assez**	entrance	**entrée**
entry	**entrée**	envelope	**enveloppe**
especially	**spécialement**	Europe	**Europe**
evening	**soir**	every	**chaque**
everything	**tout**	exactly	**exactement**
example	**exemple**	excellent	**excellent**

English	French	English	French
except	**sauf**	exchange (n)	**change**
excuse me	**pardon**	exhausted	**épuisé**
exit	**sortie**	expensive	**cher**
explain	**expliquer**	eye	**oeil**

F

F

English	French	English	French
face	**visage**	factory	**usine**
fall (v)	**tomber**	false	**faux**
family	**famille**	famous	**fameux**
fantastic	**fantastique**	far	**loin**
farm	**ferme**	fashion	**mode**
fat (adj)	**gros**	father	**père**
faucet	**robinet**	ferry	**bac**
fever	**fièvre**	few	**peu**
field	**champ**	fight (n)	**lutte**
fine	**fin**	finger	**doigt**
finish (v)	**finir**	fireworks	**feux d'artifices**
first	**premier**	first aid	**premiers secours**
first class	**première classe**	fish	**poisson**
fix (v)	**réparer**	fizzy	**pétillant**
flag	**drapeau**	flashlight	**lampe de poche**
flavor (n)	**parfum**	flea	**puce**
flight	**vol**	flower	**fleur**
flu	**grippe**	food	**nourriture**
foot	**pied**	football	**football**
for	**pour**	forbidden	**interdit**

English	French	English	French
foreign	**étranger**	forget	**oublier**
fork	**fourchette**	fountain	**fontaine**
free (no cost)	**gratuit**	French	**francais**
fresh	**fraîche**	Friday	**vendredi**
friend	**ami**	friendship	**amitié**
from	**de**	fruit	**fruit**
fun	**amusement**	funeral	**enterrement**
funny	**drôle**	furniture	**meubles**
future	**avenir**		

G

G

English	French	English	French
gallery	**gallerie**	game	**jeu**
garage	**garage**	garden	**jardin**
gas	**essence**	gas station	**station de service**
gay	**homosexuel**	gentleman	**monsieur**
genuine	**authentique**	Germany	**Allemagne**
get off	**descendre**	get out	**ficher le camp**
gift	**cadeau**	girl	**fille**
give	**donner**	glass	**verre**
glasses (eye)	**lunettes**	gloves	**gants**
go	**aller**	go away	**dégager**
God	**Dieu**	gold	**or**
golf	**golf**	good	**bien**
good-bye	**au revoir**	good day	**bonjour**
go through	**passer**	grammar	**grammaire**
grandfather	**grand-père**	grandmother	**grand-mère**
gray	**gris**	greasy	**graisseux**
great	**super**	Greece	**Grèce**
green	**vert**	grocery store	**épicerie**

English	French	English	French
guarantee	**guarantie**	guest	**invité**
guide	**guide**	guidebook	**guide**
guitar	**guitare**	gun	**fusil**

H

H

English	French	English	French
hair	**cheveux**	haircut	**coupe de cheveux**
hand	**main**	handicapped	**handicapé**
handicrafts	**produits artisanaux**	handle (n)	**poignée**
handsome	**beau**	happy	**heureux**
harbor	**port**	hard	**dûr**
hat	**chapeau**	hate (v)	**détester**
he	**il**	head	**tête**
headache	**mal de tête**	healthy	**bonne santé**
hear	**entendre**	heart	**coeur**
heat (n)	**chauffage**	heaven	**paradis**
heavy	**lourd**	hello	**bonjour**
help (n)	**secours**	her	**elle**
here	**ici**	hi	**salut**
high	**haut**	highway	**grande route**
hill	**colline**	history	**histoire**
hitchhike	**autostop**	hobby	**hobby**
hold (v)	**tenir**	hole	**trou**
holiday	**jour férié**	homemade	**fait à la maison**
homesick	**nostalgique**	honest	**honnête**
honeymoon	**lune de miel**	horrible	**horrible**
horse	**cheval**	horse riding	**équitation**
hospital	**hôpital**	hot	**chaud**

English	French	English	French
house wine	**vin de table**	how many	**combien**
how much ($)	**combien**	how	**comment**
hungry	**faim**	hurry (v)	**se dépêcher**
husband	**mari**		

I

I

English	French	English	French
I	**je**	ice cream	**glace**
ice	**glaçons**	ill	**malade**
immediately	**immédiatement**	important	**important**
imported	**importé**	impossible	**impossible**
in	**en / dans**	included	**inclus**
incredible	**incroyable**	independent	**indépendant**
indigestion	**indigestion**	industry	**industrie**
inedible	**immangeable**	information	**information**
injured	**blessé**	innocent	**innocent**
insect	**insecte**	inside	**dedans**
instant	**instant**	instead	**au lieu**
insurance	**assurance**	intelligent	**intelligent**
interesting	**intéressant**	invitation	**invitation**
is	**est**	island	**île**
Italy	**Italie**	itch (n)	**déman-geaison**

J

J

English	French	English	French
jacket	**veste**	jaw	**machoire**
jeans	**jeans**	jewelry	**bijoux**
job	**boulot**	jogging	**jogging**
joke (n)	**blague**	journey	**voyage**
juice	**jus**	jump (v)	**sauter**

English	French	English	French

K

English	French	English	French
keep	**garder**	key	**clé**
kill	**tuer**	kind	**aimable**
king	**roi**	kiss (v)	**embrasser**
kitchen	**cuisine**	knee	**genou**
knife	**couteau**	know	**savoir**

L

English	French	English	French
ladder	**échelle**	ladies	**mesdames**
lake	**lac**	lamb	**agneau**
language	**langue**	large	**grand**
last	**dernier**	late	**tard**
later	**plus tard**	laugh (v)	**rire**
laundromat	**laverie**	lawyer	**avocat**
lazy	**paresseux**	leather	**cuir**
left	**gauche**	leg	**jambe**
letter	**lettre**	library	**bibliothèque**
life	**vie**	light (n)	**lumière**
light bulb	**ampoule**	lighter (n)	**briquet**
lip	**lèvre**	list	**liste**
liter	**litre**	little (adj)	**petit**
local	**régional**	lock (v)	**fermer à clé**
lock (n)	**serrure**	lockers	**consigne**
look	**regarder**	lost	**perdu**
loud	**bruyant**	love (v)	**aimer**
lover	**amant**	low	**bas**
luck	**chance**	lungs	**poumons**

English	French	English	French
M		**M**	
macho	**macho**	mad	**fâché**
magazine	**magazine**	maggots	**asticots**
mail (n)	**courrier**	main	**principal**
make (v)	**faire**	man	**homme**
manager	**directeur**	many	**beaucoup**
map	**carte**	market	**marché**
married	**marié**	matches	**allumettes**
maximum	**maximum**	maybe	**peut-être**
meat	**viande**	medicine	**médicaments**
medium	**moyen**	men	**hommes**
menu	**carte**	message	**message**
metal	**métal**	midnight	**minuit**
mineral water	**eau minérale**	minimum	**minimum**
minutes	**minutes**	mirror	**miroir**
Miss	**Mademoiselle**	misunderstanding	**malentendu**
mix (n)	**mélange**	modern	**moderne**
moment	**moment**	Monday	**lundi**
money	**argent**	month	**mois**
monument	**monument**	moon	**lune**
more	**encore**	morning	**matin**
mosquito	**moustique**	mother	**mère**
mother-in-law	**belle mère**	mountain	**montagne**
moustache	**moustache**	mouth	**bouche**
movie	**film**	Mr.	**Monsieur**
Mrs.	**Madame**	much	**beaucoup**
muscle	**muscle**	museum	**musée**
music	**musique**	my	**mon / ma**

English	French	English	French

N

N

English	French	English	French
nail clipper	**pince à ongles**	naked	**nu**
name	**nom**	napkin	**serviette**
narrow	**étroit**	nationality	**nationalité**
natural	**naturel**	nature	**nature**
nausea	**nausée**	near	**près**
necessary	**nécessaire**	necklace	**collier**
needle	**aiguille**	nervous	**nerveux**
never	**jamais**	new	**nouveau**
newspaper	**journal**	next	**prochain**
nice	**plaisant**	nickname	**sobriquet**
night	**nuit**	no	**non**
noisy	**bruillant**	non-smoking	**non fumeur**
noon	**midi**	normal	**normale**
north	**nord**	nose	**nez**
not	**pas**	notebook	**calepin**
nothing	**rien**	no vacancy	**complet**
now	**maintenant**		

O

O

English	French	English	French
occupation	**emploi**	occupied	**occupé**
ocean	**océan**	of	**de**
office	**bureau**	oil (n)	**huile**
OK	**d'accord**	old	**vieux**
on	**sur**	once	**une fois**
one way (street)	**sens unique**	one way (ticket)	**aller simple**
only	**seulement**	open (adj)	**ouvert**
open (v)	**ouvrir**	opera	**opéra**
operator	**standardiste**	or	**ou**

English	French	English	French
orange (color)	**orange**	orange (fruit)	**orange**
original	**original**	other	**autre**
outdoors	**en plein air**	oven	**four**
over (finished)	**fini**	owner	**propriétaire**

P

P

English	French	English	French
package	**colis**	page	**page**
pail	**seau**	pain	**douleur**
painting	**tableau**	palace	**palais**
panties	**slip**	pants	**pantalon**
paper	**papier**	parents	**parents**
park (v)	**garer**	park (garden)	**parc**
party	**soirée**	passenger	**passager**
passport	**passeport**	pay	**payer**
peace	**paix**	pedestrian	**piéton**
pen	**stylo**	pencil	**crayon**
people	**gens**	pepper	**poivre**
percent	**pourcentage**	perfect	**parfait**
perfume	**parfum**	period (time)	**période**
period (woman's)	**règles**	person	**personne**
pharmacy	**pharmacie**	photo	**photo**
pick-pocket	**pickpocket**	picnic	**pique-nique**
piece	**morceau**	pig	**cochon**
pill	**pilule**	pillow	**oreiller**
pin	**épingle**	pink	**rose**
pity, it's a	**quel dommage**	pizza	**pizza**
plane	**avion**	plain	**simple**
plant	**plante**	plastic	**plastique**
plastic bag	**sac en plastique**	plate	**assiette**
platform (train)	**quai**	play (v)	**jouer**

English	French	English	French
play	**théâtre**	please	**s'il vous plaît**
pliers	**pinces**	pocket	**poche**
point (v)	**indiquer**	police	**police**
poor	**pauvre**	pork	**porc**
possible	**possible**	postcard	**carte postale**
poster	**affiche**	pot	**pot**
practical	**pratique**	pregnant	**enceinte**
prescription	**ordonnance**	present (gift)	**cadeau**
pretty	**jolie**	price	**prix**
priest	**prêtre**	prince	**prince**
princess	**princesse**	private	**privé**
problem	**problème**	prohibited	**interdit**
pronounce	**prononcer**	public	**publique**
pull	**tirer**	purple	**violet**
purse	**sac**	push	**pousser**

Q

quality	**qualité**	quarter (¼)	**quart**
queen	**reine**	question (n)	**question**
quiet	**silence**		

R

rabbit	**lapin**	radio	**radio**
railway	**chemin de fer**	rain (n)	**pluie**
rainbow	**arc-en-ciel**	raincoat	**imperméable**
rape (n)	**viol**	raw	**cru**
razor	**rasoir**	receipt	**reçu**
receive	**recevoir**	receptionist	**réceptioniste**
recipe	**recette**	recommend	**suggérer**

English	French	English	French
red	**rouge**	refill (v)	**remplir**
refund (n)	**remboursement**	relax (v)	**se reposer**
religion	**religion**	remember	**se souvenir**
rent (v)	**louer**	repair (v)	**réparer**
repeat (v)	**répéter**	reservation	**réservation**
rich	**riche**	right	**droite**
ring (n)	**bague**	ripe	**mûr**
river	**rivière**	rock (n)	**rocher**
roller skates	**patins à roulettes**	romantic	**romantique**
roof	**toit**	room	**chambre**
rope	**corde**	rotten	**pourri**
round trip	**aller-retour**	rowboat	**canot**
rucksack	**sac à dos**	rug	**tapis**
ruins	**ruines**	run (v)	**courir**

S

S

English	French	English	French
sad	**triste**	safe	**en sécurité**
sale	**solde**	same	**même**
sandals	**sandales**	sandwich	**sandwich**
sanitary napkins	**serviettes hygiéniques**	Saturday	**samedi**
scandalous	**scandaleux**	school	**école**
science	**science**	scissors	**ciseaux**
scream (v)	**crier**	screwdriver	**tournevis**
sculptor	**sculpteur**	sculpture	**sculpture**
sea	**mer**	seafood	**fruits de mer**
seat	**place**	second	**deuxième**
secret	**secret**	see	**voir**
self-service	**self-service**	sell	**vendre**
send	**envoyer**	separate (adj)	**séparé**

English	French	English	French
serious	**sérieux**	service	**service**
sex	**sexe**	sexy	**sexy**
shampoo	**shampooing**	shaving cream	**crème à raser**
she	**elle**	sheet	**drap**
shell	**coquille**	ship (n)	**navire**
shirt	**chemise**	shoes	**chaussures**
shopping	**shopping**	shore	**rive**
short	**court**	shorts	**short**
shoulder	**épaule**	show (v)	**montrer**
show (n)	**spectacle**	shower	**douche**
shy	**timide**	sick	**malade**
sign	**panneau**	silence	**silence**
silk	**soie**	silver	**argent**
similar	**semblable**	simple	**simple**
sing	**chanter**	singer	**chanteur**
sink	**lavabo**	sir	**monsieur**
sister	**soeur**	size	**taille**
ski (v)	**faire du ski**	skin	**peau**
skinny	**maigre**	skirt	**jupe**
sky	**ciel**	sleep (v)	**dormir**
sleepy	**avoir sommeil**	slice	**tranche**
slide (photo)	**diapositive**	slippery	**glissant**
slow	**lent**	small	**petit**
smell (n)	**odeur**	smile (v)	**sourire**
smoking	**fumeur**	snack	**snack**
sneeze (v)	**éternuer**	snore	**ronfler**
soap	**savon**	socks	**chaussettes**
something	**quelque chose**	son	**fils**
song	**chanson**	soon	**bientôt**
sorry	**désolé**	sour	**aigre**
south	**sud**	speak	**parler**

English	French	English	French
specialty	**spécialité**	speed	**vitesse**
spend	**dépenser**	spider	**araignée**
spoon	**cuillère**	sport	**sport**
spring	**printemps**	square	**place**
stairs	**escalier**	stamp	**timbre**
star (in sky)	**étoile**	state	**état**
station	**station**	stomach	**estomac**
stone	**caillou**	stop (n)	**stop / arrêt**
stop (v)	**arrêter**	storm	**tempête**
story (floor)	**étage**	straight	**droit**
strange (odd)	**bizarre**	stream (n)	**ruisseau**
street	**rue**	string	**ficelle**
strong	**fort**	stuck	**coincé**
student	**étudiant**	stupid	**stupide**
sturdy	**robuste**	style	**mode**
suddenly	**soudain**	suitcase	**valise**
summer	**été**	sun	**soleil**
sunbathe	**se faire bronzer**	sunburn	**coup de soleil**
Sunday	**dimanche**	sunglasses	**lunettes de soleil**
sunny	**ensoleillé**	sunset	**coucher de soleil**
sun screen	**lotion solaire**	sunshine	**soleil**
sunstroke	**insolation**	suntan (n)	**bronzage**
suntan lotion	**huile solaire**	supermarket	**supermarché**
supplement	**supplément**	surprise (n)	**surprise**
swallow (v)	**avaler**	sweat (v)	**transpirer**
sweater	**pull**	sweet	**doux**
swim	**nager**	swimming pool	**piscine**
swim suit	**costume de bain**	swim trunks	**maillot de bain**

English	French	English	French
Switzerland	**Suisse**	synthetic	**synthétique**

T   ## T

English	French	English	French
table	**table**	tail	**queue**
take out (food)	**emporter**	take	**prendre**
talcum powder	**talc**	talk	**parler**
tall	**grand**	tampons	**tampons**
tape (cassette)	**cassette**	taste (n)	**goût**
taste (v)	**goûter**	tax	**taxe**
teacher	**professeur**	team	**équipe**
teenager	**adolescent**	telephone	**téléphone**
television	**télévision**	temperature	**température**
tender	**tendre**	tennis shoes	**chaussures de tennis**
tent	**tente**	terrible	**terrible**
thanks	**merci**	theater	**théâtre**
thermometer	**thermomètre**	thick	**épais**
thief	**voleur**	thigh	**cuisse**
thin	**mince**	thing	**chose**
think	**penser**	thirsty	**soif**
thread	**fil**	throat	**gorge**
through	**à travers**	throw	**jeter**
Thursday	**jeudi**	ticket	**billet**
tight	**serré**	timetable	**horaire**
tired	**fatigué**	tissues	**papier-linge**
to	**à**	today	**aujourd'hui**
toe	**orteil**	together	**ensemble**
toilet paper	**papier hygiénique**	toilet	**toilette**
tomorrow	**demain**	tonight	**ce soir**
too	**trop**	tool	**outil**

English	French	English	French
tooth	**dent**	toothbrush	**brosse à dents**
toothpaste	**dentifrice**	toothpick	**cure-dent**
total	**total**	touch (v)	**toucher**
tough	**dur**	tour	**tour**
tourist	**touriste**	towel	**serviette de bain**
tower	**tour**	town	**village**
toy	**jouet**	track (train)	**voie ferrée**
traditional	**traditionnel**	traffic	**circulation**
train	**train**	translate	**traduire**
travel	**voyager**	travel agency	**agence de voyage**
travelers check	**chèque de voyage**	tree	**arbre**
trip	**voyage**	trouble	**trouble**
T-shirt	**T-shirt**	Tuesday	**mardi**
tunnel	**tunnel**	turn (v)	**tourner**
tweezers	**pince à épiler**	twins	**jumeaux**

U

U

English	French	English	French
ugly	**laid**	umbrella	**parapluie**
under	**sous**	underpants	**slip**
understand	**comprendre**	underwear	**sous vêtements**
unemployed	**au chômage**	unfortunately	**malheureusement**
United States	**Etats-Unis**	university	**univerisité**
up	**en haut**	upstairs	**en haut**
urgent	**urgent**	us	**nous**

English	French	English	French
use	**utiliser**		

V

V

vacant	**libre**	vacancy (hotel)	**chambre libre**
valley	**vallée**	vegetarian (n)	**végétarien**
very	**très**	vest	**gilet**
video	**vidéo**	video recorder	**magnéto-scope**
view	**vue**	village	**village**
vineyard	**vignoble**	virus	**virus**
visit (n)	**visite**	vitamins	**vitamines**
voice	**voix**	vomit (v)	**vomir**

W

W

waist	**taille**	wait	**attendre**
waiter	**garçon**	waitress	**serveuse**
wake up	**se réveiller**	walk (v)	**marcher**
wallet	**portefeuille**	want	**vouloir**
warm (adj)	**chaud**	wash	**laver**
watch (v)	**regarder**	watch (n)	**montre**
water	**eau**	water, tap	**eau du robinet**
waterfall	**cascade**	we	**nous**
weather forecast	**météo**	weather	**temps**
wedding	**mariage**	Wednesday	**mercredi**
week	**semaine**	weight	**poids**
welcome	**bienvenue**	west	**ouest**
wet	**mouillé**	what	**que**
wheel	**roue**	when	**quand**

English	French	English	French
where	**où**	whipped cream	**crème chantilly**
white	**blanc**	who	**qui**
why	**pourquoi**	widow	**veuve**
widower	**veuf**	wife	**femme**
wild	**sauvage**	wind	**vent**
window	**fenêtre**	wine	**vin**
wing	**aile**	winter	**hiver**
wire (money)	**télégraphier**	wish (v)	**souhaiter**
with	**avec**	without	**sans**
women	**dames**	wood	**bois**
wool	**laine**	word	**mot**
work (n)	**travail**	world	**monde**
worse	**pire**	worst	**le pire**
wrap	**emballer**	wrist	**poignet**
write	**écrire**		

Y

Y

English	French	English	French
year	**année**	yellow	**jaune**
yes	**oui**	yesterday	**hier**
you (formal)	**vous**	you (informal)	**tu**
young	**jeune**	youth hostel	**auberge de jeunesse**

Z

Z

English	French	English	French
zero	**zero**	zipper	**fermeture éclair**
zoo	**zoo**		

Hurdling the Language Barrier

Don't be afraid to communicate

Even the best phrase book won't satisfy your needs in every situation. To really hurdle the language barrier, you need to leap beyond the printed page, and dive into contact with the locals. Never, never, never allow your lack of foreign language skills to isolate you from the people and cultures you traveled halfway 'round the world to experience. Remember that in every country you visit, you're surrounded by expert, native-speaking tutors. Spend bus and train rides letting them teach you. Always start a conversation by asking politely, "Do you speak English?"

When you communicate in English with someone from another country, speak slowly, clearly, and with carefully chosen words. Use what the Voice of America calls "simple English." You're talking to people who are wishing it was written down, hoping to see each letter as it tumbles out of your mouth. Pronounce each letter, avoiding all contractions and slang. For bad examples, listen to other tourists.

Keep things caveman-simple. Make single nouns work as entire sentences ("Photo?"). Use internationally understood words ("auto kaput" works in Sicily). Butcher the language if you must. The important thing is to make the effort. To get air mail stamps you can flap your wings and say "tweet, tweet, tweet." If you want milk, moo and pull two imaginary udders. Risk looking like a fool (remind yourself that you'll probably never see these people again).

Go ahead and make educated guesses. Many situations are easy-to-fake multiple choice questions. Practice. Read timetables, concert posters and newspaper headlines. Listen to each language on a multi-lingual tour. Be melodramatic. Exaggerate the local accent. Self-consciousness is the deadliest communication-killer.

Choose multi-lingual people to communicate with, like business people, urbanites, young well-dressed people, or anyone in the tourist trade. Use a small note pad to keep track of handy phrases you pick up -- and to help you communicate more clearly with the locals by scribbling down numbers, maps, and so on. Some travelers carry important messages written on a small card (vegetarian, boiled water, your finest ice cream, and so on).

Easy cultural bugaboos to avoid

- When writing numbers, give your sevens a cross (7) and give your ones an upswing (1).
- European dates are different: Christmas is 25-12-94, not 12-25-94.
- Commas are decimal points and decimals are commas, so a dollar and a half is 1,50 and there are 5.280 feet in a mile.
- The European "first floor" is not the ground floor, but the first floor up.
- When counting with your fingers, start with your thumb. If you hold up only your first finger, you'll probably get two of something.

French tongue twisters

Tongue twisters are a great way to practice a language -- and break the ice with local Europeans. Here are a few French tongue twisters that are sure to challenge you, and amuse your hosts.

Bonjour madame la saucissonière! Combien sont ces six saucissons-ci? Ces six saucissons-ci sont six sous. Si ces saucissons-ci sont six sous, ces six saucissons-ci sont trop chers.

Hello madame sausage-seller! How much are these six sausages? These six sausages here are six cents. If these here are six cents, these six sausages are too expensive.

Je veux et j'exige qu'un chasseur sachant chasser sans ses èchasses sache chasser sans son chien de chasse.

I want and demand that a hunter who knows how to hunt without his stilts knows how to hunt without his hunting dog.

Ce sont seize cent jacynthes sèches dans seize cent sachets secs.

There are 600 dry hyacinths in 600 dry sachets.

Ce sont trois très gros rats dans trois très gros trous roulant trois gros rats gris morts.

There are three fat rats in three fat rat-holes rolling three fat grey dead rats.

English tongue twisters

After your French friends have laughed at you, let them try these tongue twisters in English.

The sixth sick sheik's sixth sheep's sick.

One smart fellow he felt smart, two smart fellows they felt smart, three smart fellows they all felt smart.

I'm a pleasant mother pheasant plucker. I pluck mother pheasants. I'm the most pleasant mother peasant plucker that ever plucked a mother pheasant.

International words

As our world shrinks, more and more words hop across their linguistic boundaries and become international. Savvy travelers develop a knack for choosing words most likely to be universally understood ("auto" instead of "car," "kaput" rather than "broken," "photo," not "picture"). They also internationalize their pronunciation. "University," if you play around with its sound (oo-nee-vehr-see-tay) will be understood anywhere. Practice speaking English with a heavy French accent. Wave your arms a lot. Be creative.

Here are a few internationally understood words. Remember, cut out the Yankee accent and give each word a pan-European sound.

Stop	Kaput	Vino	Restaurant
Ciao	Bank	Hotel	Bye-bye
Rock 'n roll	Post	Camping	OK
Auto	Picnic	Amigo	Autobus (boos)
Nuclear	Macho	Tourist	English (Engleesh)
Yankee	Americano	Mama mia	Michelangelo
Beer	Oo la la	Coffee	Casanova (romantic)
Chocolate	Moment	Sexy	Disneyland
Tea	Coca-Cola	No problem	Mañana
Telephone	Photo	Photocopy	Passport
Europa	Self-service	Toilet	Police
Super	Taxi	Central	Information
Pardon	University	Fascist	Rambo
American profanity			

French Gestures

Gestures say a lot

In your travels, gestures can either raise or lower the language barrier. For instance, pointing to your head can mean smart in one country and crazy in another. And if you shake your head "no" in Bulgaria, you've just said "yes." Gesture boundaries often follow linguistic ones, but not always. Occasionally a gesture which is very popular in one town or region is meaningless or has a completely different meaning a few miles away. Here are a few common French gestures and their meanings:

The Fingertips Kiss: Gently bring the fingers and thumb of your right hand together, raise to your lips, kiss lightly, and toss your fingers and thumb into the air. Be careful, tourists look silly when they over-emphasize this subtle action.

It can mean sexy, delicious, divine, or wonderful.

The Eyelid Pull: Place your extended forefinger below the center of your eye, and pull the skin downward.

In France this means "I am alert. I'm looking. You can't fool me."

The Roto-Wrist: Hold your forearm out from your waist with your open palm down, and pivot your wrist clockwise and counter-clockwise like you're opening a doorknob.

When a Frenchman uses this gesture while explaining something to you, he isn't sure of the information -- or it's complete B.S.

The Chin Flick: Tilt your head back slightly, and flick the back of your fingers forward in an arc from under your chin.

In France and Italy this means "I'm not interested, you bore me," or "You bother me."

The Forearm Jerk: Clench your right fist, and jerk your forearm up as you slap your bicep with your left palm.

This is a rude phallic gesture that men throughout southern Europe often use the way Americans give someone "the finger." This extra-large version says "I'm superior" (it's an action some monkeys actually do with their penis to insult their peers).

The Hand Purse: Straighten the fingers and thumb of one hand, bringing them all together to make an upward point. Your hands can be held still or moved a little up and down at the wrist.

This very Italian gesture is sometimes used by the French to mean "fear."

To beckon someone: Remember that in northern Europe you bring your palm up, and in France and the south you wave it down. To Americans this often looks like "go away" -- not the invitation it really is.

Let's Talk Telephones

Understanding those Francophones

You can usually make a long-distance phone call from a French PTT (post office), but it's quicker, easier and no more expensive to use the public phones on the street.

A super-efficient, vandal-resistant card-operated system is rapidly replacing France's coin-operated public phone system. You'll still find the soon-to-be-extinct coin phones in smaller cities. The coin phones are self-explanatory, usually with English instructions for international calls. To call the USA, drop in a 5F coin, dial 19-1-area code-number, and you're in business (for 20 seconds anyway).

The coin-free card system is even easier. Buy a *télécarte* (French phone card), available at any PTT, tourist office, train station, and most *tabac* shops. The smallest value is 40F. The price of a call, local or international, will automatically be deducted from your card as you use it. To use the *télécarte* phone booths, follow the instructions that will prompt you to: (1) *decrochez* (pick up the receiver); (2) *inserez votre carte* (insert your card); (3) *fermez le volet* (close the lid over the card -- not required on newer machines); (4) *patientez* (wait a few seconds); and (5) *composez votre numero* (dial your number). Buy a *télécarte* at the beginning of your trip and use it for hotel reservations, tourist information, and phoning home.

France has basically no area codes. You dial the 8-

digit telephone number direct throughout the country. The only exception is calling into or out of Paris. From Paris you must dial 16 to get a long-distance line for calls within France. To dial Paris from elsewhere in France, you must dial 16-1, then the eight-digit number. To and from other cities, simply dial the eight-digit number listed. To reach France from another country, dial the French country code (33) and the eight-digit number (or "1" plus eight digits for Paris).

Country codes
To call out of France, dial 19, country code, area code (without zero prefix), local number.

France:	33	Germany:	49	USA/Canada:	1
Austria:	43	Britain:	44	Switzerland:	41
Belgium:	32	Italy:	39	Netherlands:	31
Spain:	34				

Advantages of USA calling cards
If you plan to call home often, get an ATT, MCI or SPRINT calling card. This lets you dial up a special toll-free operator who takes your card number and the number you want to call, puts you through, and bills your home telephone number at the cheap USA rate of about $1 per minute plus a flat service charge of around $2.50. If you talk for at least 3 minutes, you'll save enough to make up for the service charge.

Special USA calling card operators in France

ATT: 19 (dial tone) 00-11
MCI: 19 (dial tone) 0019
SPRINT: 19 (dial tone) 0087

Useful Parisian phone numbers and addresses

English tourist info recording: 47-20-88-98
American Express: 11 Rue Scribe (métro: Opera) 42-66-09-99
American Church: 47-05-07-99
American Hospital: 47-47-53-00
American Pharmacy: 47-42-49-40
Emergency: Dial 17 for police, otherwise 42-60-33-22
Office of American Services: 42-96-12-02 (lost passports, etc.)
U.S. Embassy: 42-96-12-02
Directory Assistance: 12 (they speak some English)
Sunday banks: 115 & 154 Ave. des Champs-Élysées

Orly airport info: 48-84-32-10 or 49-75-15-15
Roissy-Ch. de Gaulle airport: 48-62-22-80
Air France: 43-35-61-61
American: 42-89-05-22
British Air: 47-78-14-14
Continental: 42-25-31-81
Delta: 43-35-40-80
KLM: 42-66-45-45
Northwest: 42-66-90-00
SAS: 47-42-06-14
TWA: 47-60-62-11
United: 48-97-82-82

City	Tourist info	Train info	Postal code (zip)
Rouen	35-71-41-77	35-98-50-50	76000
Honfleur	31-89-15-53	call tourist office	14600
Bayeux	31-92-16-26	31-92-80-50	14400
Mont St. Michel	33-30-14-30	33-60-10-97 (bus)	50016
Amboise	47-57-09-28	47-20-50-50	37400
Brantôme	53-05-80-52	call tourist office	
Sarlat	53-59-27-67	53-90-00-21	24200
Albi	63-54-22-30	63-54-50-50	81000
Carcassonne	68-25-07-04	68-47-50-50	11000
Arles	90-96-29-35	90-93-74-90 (bus)	13200
Avignon	90-82-65-11	09-82-50-50	84000
Nice	93-87-07-07	98-87-50-50	06000
Chamonix	50-53-00-24	50-53-00-44	74400
Beaune	80-22-24-51	80-44-50-50	21200
Dijon	80-43-42-12	80-41-50-50	21000
Colmar	89-41-02-29	89-41-66-80	68000
Verdun	29-84-18-85	29-86-25-65	55100
Reims	26-88-37-89	26-88-50-50	51084
Paris	47-23-61-72 (almost always busy)	several stations (often do not speak English)	750XX (last 2 digits are arrondissement)

Weather

First line is average daily low (°F.); 2nd line average daily high (°F.); 3rd line, days of no rain.

	J	F	M	A	M	J	J	A	S	O	N	D
Paris	32	34	36	41	47	52	55	55	50	44	38	33
	42	45	52	60	67	73	76	75	69	59	49	43
	16	15	16	16	18	19	19	19	19	17	15	14
Nice	40	41	45	49	56	62	66	66	62	55	48	43
	56	56	59	64	69	76	81	81	77	70	62	58
	23	20	23	23	23	25	29	26	24	22	23	23

Metric conversions (approximate)

1 inch = 25 millimeters   1 foot = .3 meter
1 yard = .9 meter   1 mile = 1.6 kilometers
1 sq. yard = .8 sq. meter   1 acre = 0.4 hectare
1 quart = .95 liter   1 ounce = 28 grams
1 pound = .45 kilo   1 kilo = 2.2 pounds
1 centimeter = 0.4 inch   1 meter = 39.4 inches
    36-24-36 = 90-60-90

1 kilometer = .62 mile
Miles = kilometers divided by 2 plus 10%
(120 km/2 = 60, 60 +12 = 72 miles)

Fahrenheit degrees = double Celsius + 30
32° F = 0° C, 82° F = about 28° C

Your tear-out cheat sheet

Keep this sheet of the most essential French words and phrases in your pocket. That way you can memorize them during idle moments, or quickly refer to them if you're caught without your phrase book.

The ten essentials:

Good day.	**Bonjour.**	bohn-zhoor
Do you speak English?	**Parlez-vous anglais?**	par-lay-voo ahn-gleh
Yes.	**Oui.**	wee
No.	**Non.**	nohn
I don't understand.	**Je ne comprends pas.**	zhuh nuh kohn-prahn pah
I'm sorry.	**Je regrette.**	zhuh ruh-greht
Please.	**S'il vous plaît.**	see voo pleh
Thanks.	**Merci.**	mehr-see
Thank you very much.	**Merci beaucoup.**	mehr-see boh-koo
Goodbye.	**Au revoir.**	oh ruh-vwahr

Where?

Where is...?	**Où est...?**	oo eh
...a hotel	**...un hôtel**	uhn oh-tehl
...a youth hostel	**...une auberge de jeunesse**	ewn oh-behrzh duh zhuh-nehs
...a restaurant	**...un restaurant**	uhn rehs-toh-rahn
...a grocery store	**...une épicerie**	ewn ay-pee-suh-ree
...the train station	**...la gare**	lah gar

...the tourist information office	...**l'office du tourisme**	loh-fees dew too-reez-muh
...the toilet	...**la toilette**	lah twah-leht
men / women	**hommes / dames**	ohm / dahm

How much?

How much?	**Combien?**	kohn-bee-an
Will you write it down?	**Pouvez-vous l'écrire?**	poo-vay-voo lay-kreer
Cheap.	**Bon marché.**	bohn mar-shay
Cheaper.	**Moins cher.**	mwan shehr
Included?	**Inclus?**	an-klew
I would like...	**Je voudrais...**	zhuh voo-dreh
We would like...	**Nous voudrions...**	noo voo-dree-ohn
Just a little.	**Un petit peu.**	uhn puh-tee puh
More.	**Encore.**	ahn-kor
A ticket.	**Un billet.**	uhn bee-yeh
A room.	**Une chambre.**	ewn shahn-bruh
The bill.	**L'addition.**	lah-dee-see-ohn

One through ten:

one	**un**	uhn
two	**deux**	duh
three	**trois**	trwah
four	**quatre**	kah-truh
five	**cinq**	sank
six	**six**	sees
seven	**sept**	seht
eight	**huit**	weet
nine	**neuf**	nuhf
ten	**dix**	dees

The Europe Through the Back Door Catalog

All of these items have been specially designed for independent budget travelers. They have been thoroughly field tested by Rick Steves and his globe-trotting ETBD staff, and are completely guaranteed. Prices include shipping, tax, and a free subscription to our quarterly newsletter/catalog.

Back Door Bag convertible suitcase/backpack $70

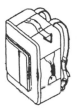 At 9"x21"x13" this specially-designed, sturdy, functional bag is maximum carry-on-the-plane size (fits under the seat), and your key to foot-loose and fancy-free travel. Made from rugged, water-resistant Cordura nylon, it converts from a smart-looking suitcase to a handy backpack. It has hide-away padded shoulder straps, top and side handles, and a detachable shoulder strap (for toting as a suitcase). Lockable perimeter zippers allow easy access to the roomy (2500 cubic inches) central compartment. Two large outside pockets are perfect for frequently used items. Also included is one nylon stuff bag. Over 40,000 Back Door travelers have used these bags around the world. Rick Steves helped design this bag, and lives out of it for 3 months at a time. Comparable bags cost much more. Available in black, grey, navy blue and teal green.

Eurailpasses

...cost the same everywhere, but only ETBD gives you
a free 90-minute "How to get the most out of your
railpass" video, free advice on your itinerary, and your
choice of one of Rick Steves' "22 Day" books. No
wonder why ETBD has become the second largest
Eurailpass retailer in the USA. It's easy to order your
pass by mail -- call 206/771-8303, and we'll send you a
full description of the types of Eurailpasses available,
pass prices, our unique map for comparing Eurail and
pay-as-you-go rail prices, and our user-friendly
Eurailpass order form.

Moneybelt $8

Absolutely required no matter where you're traveling!
An ultra-light, sturdy, under-the-pants, one-size-fits-all
nylon pouch, our svelte moneybelt is just the right size
to carry your passport, airline tickets and traveler's
checks comfortably. Made to ETBD's specifications,
this moneybelt is your best defense against theft --
when you wear it, feeling a Gypsy's hand in your
pocket will become just another interesting cultural
experience.

*Prices are good through 1993. Orders will be processed
within 2 weeks. For rush orders (which we process within
48 hours), please add $10. Send your check to:*

Europe Through the Back Door

109 Fourth Ave. N, PO Box 2009
Edmonds, WA 98020

More books by Rick Steves...
*Now more than ever, travelers are determined to get the
most out of every mile, minute and dollar. That's what
Rick's books are all about. He'll help you have a better trip
because you're on a budget, not in spite of it. Each of these
books is published by John Muir Publications, and is
available through your local bookstore, or the Europe
Through the Back Door newsletter/catalog.*

Europe Through The Back Door
Now in its 11th edition, *ETBD* has given thousands of
people the skills and confidence they needed to travel
through the less-touristed "back doors" of Europe.
You'll find chapters on packing, itinerary-planning,
transportation, finding rooms, travel photography,
keeping safe and healthy, plus individual chapters on
Rick's 40 favorite back door discoveries. 1993 edition.

**Mona Winks: Self-Guided Tours of Europe's
Top Museums**
Let's face it, museums can ruin a good vacation. But
Mona Winks takes you by the hand, giving you fun
and easy-to-follow self-guided tours through Europe's
20 most frightening and exhausting museums and
cultural obligations. Packed with more than 200 maps
and illustrations. 1993 edition.

Europe 101: History and Art for the Traveler
A lively, entertaining crash course in European history
and art, *101* is the perfect way to prepare yourself for
the rich cultural smorgasbord that awaits you.

2 to 22 Days in Europe
2 to 22 Days in Great Britain
2 to 22 Days in France
2 to 22 Days in Italy
2 to 22 Days in Germany, Austria & Switzerland
2 to 22 Days in Norway, Sweden & Denmark
2 to 22 Days in Spain & Portugal

Planning an itinerary can be the most difficult and important part of a trip -- and you haven't even left yet. To get you started, Rick gives you a day-by-day plan linking his favorite places in Europe, complete with maps, descriptions of sights, and recommended places to stay. Some people follow a 22-day route to the letter, and others use it as a general outline. Either way, your *2 to 22 days in...* guidebook will help you structure your trip so you'll get the most out of every moment. These guides are updated every year.

Europe Through the Back Door Phrase Books:
French, Italian and German

Finally, a series of phrase books written specially for the budget traveler! Each book gives you the words, phrases and easy-to-use phonetics you need to communicate with the locals about room-finding, transportation, food, health -- you'll even learn how to start conversations about politics, philosophy and romance -- all spiced with Rick Steves' travel tips, and his unique blend of down-to-earth practicality and humor. All are 1993 editions.

What we do at Europe Through the Back Door

At ETBD we value travel as a powerful way to better
understand and contribute to the world in which we
live. Our mission at ETBD is to equip travelers with
the confidence and skills necessary to travel through
Europe independently, economically, and in a way
that is culturally broadening. To accomplish this, we:
Teach do-it-yourself travel seminars (often for free);
Research and write guidebooks to Europe and a public
    television series;
Sell Eurailpasses, our favorite guidebooks, maps,
    travel bags, and other travelers' supplies;
Provide travel consulting services;
Organize and lead unique Back Door tours of Europe;
Sponsor our Travel Resource Center in Edmonds, WA;
...and we travel a lot.

Back Door 'Best of Europe' tours

If you like our independent travel philosophy but
would like to benefit from the camaraderie and
efficiency of group travel, our Back Door tours may be
right up your alley. Every year we lead friendly,
intimate 'Best of Europe in 22 Days' tours, free-spirited
'Un-Tours' and special regional tours of Turkey,
Britain, France and other places that we especially
love. For details, dates and prices, call 206/771-8303
and ask for our free newsletter/catalog.

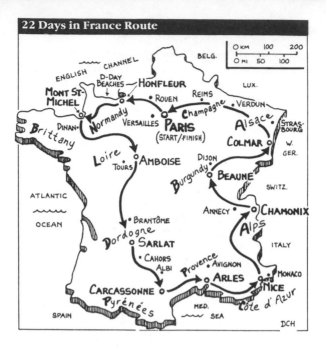

22 Days in France Route

You've got your phrase book, but have you planned your itinerary yet?

If this route looks good to you, pick up a copy of Rick Steves' *2 to 22 Days in France*. You'll get the most productive day-by-day itinerary through France, with up-to-date listings of Rick's favorite budget accomodations along the way.

Reader feedback pages

Your feedback will do a lot to improve future editions of this phrase book. To help tomorrow's travelers travel smarter, please use the blank pages at the end of this book to jot down ideas, phrases, and suggestions as they hit you during your travels, and then send them to me. Merci!

Rick Steves
Europe Through the Back Door
109 Fourth Ave. N, PO Box 2009
Edmonds, WA 98020

Other Great Travel Books by Rick Steves

Asia Through the Back Door, 3rd ed., 326 pp. $15.95 (4th ed. avail. 6/93 $16.95)

Europe 101: History & Art for the Traveler, 4th ed., 372 pp. $15.95

Europe Through the Back Door, 11th ed., 432 pp. $17.95

Europe Through the Back Door Phrase Book: German, 168 pp. $4.95

Europe Through the Back Door Phrase Book: Italian, 168 pp. $4.95

Mona Winks: Self-Guided Tours of Europe's Top Museums, 2nd ed., 456 pp. $16.95

2 to 22 Days in Europe, 1993 ed., 288 pp. $13.95

2 to 22 Days in France, 1993 ed., 192 pp. $10.95

2 to 22 Days in Germany, Austria, & Switzerland, 1993 ed., 224 pp. $10.95

2 to 22 Days in Great Britain, 1993 ed., 192 pp. $10.95

2 to 22 Days in Italy, 1993 ed., 208 pp. $10.95

2 to 22 Days in Norway, Sweden, & Denmark, 1993 ed., 192 pp. $10.95

2 to 22 Days in Spain & Portugal, 1993 ed., 192 pp. $10.95

Kidding Around Seattle: A Young Person's Guide to the City, 64 pp. $9.95 (Ages 8 and up)

More European Travel Books Available from John Muir Publications

Great Cities of Eastern Europe, 256 pp. $16.95

Opera! The Guide to Western Europe's Great Houses, 296 pp. $18.95

22 Days Around the World, 1993 ed., 264 pp. $13.95

Understanding Europeans, 272 pp. $14.95

Undiscovered Islands of the Mediterranean, 2nd ed., 256 pp. $10.95

A Viewer's Guide to Art: A Glossary of Gods, People, and Creatures, 144 pp. $10.95

For Young Readers Traveling Abroad, Consider Our "Kidding Around" Travel Guides (Ages 8 and up)

Kidding Around London, 64 pp. $9.95

Kidding Around Paris,
64 pp. $9.95
Kidding Around Spain,
108 pp. $12.95

These are just a sampling of the many titles we have to offer. Whether you are traveling within the U.S. or around the world, turn to John Muir Publications for unique travel titles to practically any location.

Call or write for our *free* catalog listing our complete selection of travel and young readers titles. All the necessary information is listed below.

Ordering Information

If you cannot find our books in your local bookstore, you can order directly from us. If you send us money for a book not yet available, we will hold your money until we can ship you the book. Your books will be sent to you via UPS (for U.S. destinations). UPS will not deliver to a P.O. Box; please give us a street address. Include $3.75 for the first item ordered and $.50 for each additional item to cover shipping and handling costs.

For airmail within the U.S., enclose $4.00. All foreign orders will be shipped surface rate; please enclose $3.00 for the first item and $1.00 for each additional item. Please inquire about foreign airmail rates.

Method of Payment

Your order may be paid by check, money order, or credit card. We cannot be responsible for cash sent through the mail. All payments must be made in U.S. dollars drawn on a U.S. bank. Canadian postal money orders in U.S. dollars are acceptable. For VISA, MasterCard, or American Express orders, include your card number, expiration date, and your signature, or call **(800) 888-7504**. Books ordered on American Express cards can be shipped only to the billing address of the cardholder. Sorry, no C.O.D.'s. Residents of sunny New Mexico, add 6.125% tax to the total.

Address all orders and inquiries to:
> **John Muir Publications**
> **P.O. Box 613**
> **Santa Fe, NM 87504**
> **(505) 982-4078**
> **(800) 888-7504**